Praise for *Utterly Wicked*

"I cannot say enough about *Utterly Wicked!* If I were to describe this book, I would call it utterly amazing, utterly thorough, and utterly potent. Dorothy explores the side of magic that is talked about more in whispers than it is spoken about openly. She has done a phenomenal job in showing the reader practical applications that will enable them to send their worst enemy to hell and look forward to the trip! *Utterly Wicked* is filled with priceless knowledge that any practitioner of magic should have. From rats to roaches, hair to fingernails, this book has it all!

I cannot recommend *Utterly Wicked* highly enough to anyone that has a desire to learn. The power in this magical writing is one that will bring change to both readers and their enemies!" —**Hoodoo Sen Moise,** author of *Working Conjure*

"Find and own your shadow in the way of the witches of old. Truthful and uncompromising, *Utterly Wicked* is a book *every* witch should read, simply to know what's out there, even if you decide you never need to use it. Cheers to Dorothy Morrison for tackling this unpopular but very important and misunderstood subject." —**Christopher Penczak,** bestselling author and founder of the Temple of Witchcraft

"Here is a book that bravely reveals the old authentic arts of the Craft in a way that is best suited for the modern practitioner. The material is bold and frank, sure to boil your cauldron's brew." —**Raven Grimassi,** author of *What We Knew in the Night*

"Empowering and invigorating, *Utterly Wicked* is true to its title as it contains an array of fiercely shrewd and cunning magical spells of justified revenge for every imaginable circumstance. It is also brimming with an abundance of recipes to make oils, powders, and washes not only for cursing purposes but for self-confidence, protection, and more! After having read this book, it is clearly apparent that Dorothy Morrison is an exceptionally devoted teacher. Most impressive, however, is her ongoing compassionate concern for her readers' psychological and spiritual well-being. This book is, without a doubt, a treasure chest of precious informa— —Miss Aida, author of *Hoodoo Cleansing and Protection Magic*

"Sassy, wise, and wonderful, Dorothy Morrison's *Utterly Wicked* opens the gateway into a witchcraft garden that has been largely ignored. This book is filled with creative ideas for turning the tables, declaring personal agency, and correcting life's little quagmires. Highly recommended by this village witch— go buy it!" —**H. Byron Ballard,** author of *Earth Works*

"*Utterly Wicked* is top shelf material for any Hoodoo or witch, in training or not." —**Stephanie Rose Bird,** author of *Sticks, Stones, Roots, and Bones* and *Out of the Blue*

"Dorothy Morrison is a wonderfully magickal powerhouse. *Utterly Wicked* is a groundbreaking and necessary work that tells honest truths and, more importantly, provides strong solutions for every eventuality. It is a must-have for any spiritual person worth their salt." —**Lilith Dorsey,** author of *Love Magic*

"Dorothy Morrison knows that, in real witchcraft wars, you don't bring beach sand to a graveyard dirt fight. Yet, protection and defense are two aspects of modern-day witchcraft that are often misunderstood. Whether a neophyte or an adept in the magickal arts, I highly recommend Dorothy Morrison's *Utterly Wicked* as the perfect introduction to this body of knowledge. It is a book for those individuals who are tired of being the victim, who are interested in settling the score and leveling the playing field. It contains spells and techniques designed to arm the practicing witch with the ability to deal with life on life's terms—the good, the bad, and the downright ugly. But Morrison also schools her readers about the nature of curses and hexes, and explains how they have more than a singular application. It's not always about harm and destruction. It is also about eliminating obstructions and neutralizing enemies. It is about turning evil and naysayers on their heads. It is about finding justice in a world full of injustices. And sometimes a simple binding is not enough. Sometimes, people need to be stopped dead in their tracks. Indeed, there is a belief among adepts that a witch should never fear a situation when armed with the knowledge and skill that is their craft, because they know that the most frightening thing in every nightmare is the witch. For Morrison, the well-armed witch is one who is prepared to traverse the nightmare. After reading *Utterly Wicked*, it will become abundantly clear that Dorothy Morrison is 100 percent *that witch,* and she will show you how to be that witch, too." —**Denise Alvarado,** author of *The Magic of Marie Laveau* and *The Voodoo Hoodoo Spellbook*

DOROTHY MORRISON

UTTERLY WICKED

Hexes, Curses, and Other Unsavory Notions

with a foreword by Amy Blackthorn, author of *Blackthorn's Botanical Magic*

WEISER BOOKS

This edition first published in 2020 by Weiser Books, an imprint of
Red Wheel/Weiser, LLC
With offices at:
65 Parker Street, Suite 7
Newburyport, MA 01950
www.redwheelweiser.com

ISBN: 978-1-57863-696-9
Library of Congress Cataloging-in-Publication Data
available upon request.

Cover design by Kathryn Sky-Peck
Cover artwork by Sabrina the Ink Witch
Interior by Steve Amarillo / Urban Design LLC
Typeset in Adobe Sabon, Optima and Monotype Tusar Deco

Printed in the United States of America
IBI
10 9 8 7 6 5 4 3 2 1

For Jonathon Minton, who on more occasions
than I can count has kept me safe and sane,
and who on more occasions than he'll ever
know has saved a good portion of the world
from becoming green, warty, and ribbety.

IN MEMORY OF
Ken Valieu, who would have been just as
excited about this book as I am—and Velvet
Rieth, who witnessed the worst of my cursing,
both magical and otherwise, and still loved me
in spite of it. I miss you both!

And . . .

IN MEMORY OF
All those folks who once called me
whitesy-lightsy.
(They should've known better!)

Contents

Foreword

You dear reader, are holding a treasure. A treasure by a woman who is not only an incredible writer, but one who has been bringing her humor and utterly fabulous brand of witchcraft to us for decades. I have adored Dorothy Morrison's books since the late '90s, but my connection to this one is particularly special.

In the summer of 2007, I was working at a shop called Mystickal Voyage, teaching classes on topics ranging from folk magic to herbal spellcraft and reading tarot for clients. I was thrilled to hear that Dorothy would be publishing another book. Reading the promotional material for *Utterly Wicked*, I was eagerly anticipating its release and started mentioning it to others in the shop.

You see, in late 2005 after the devastation of Hurricane Katrina, Dorothy, among other prominent Pagans, got together to auction off items with the proceeds going to Hurricane Katrina charities. I was the winning bidder of a one-of-a-kind piece—a Book of Shadows by the lovely Dorothy Morrison. This beautiful book arrived at my home as a ream of printed parchment with the title page autographed by the author. I was thrilled to have not only materials from other books I enjoyed but unreleased materials as well. I hoped that some of the unreleased material would appear in *Utterly Wicked*. When Ms. Morrison later appeared at Mystickal Voyage on tour for this book, I made sure to bring the massive Book of Shadows with me, to thank her again. Dorothy was the first person I thought of when seeking endorsements for my first book, *Blackthorn's Botanical Magic*. She was also the first to respond.

Dorothy doesn't just understand the practices laid out in these pages, she writes from a deep well of knowledge and practice. At Mystickal Voyage, we had adjourned outside during her break between tarot clients to catch up and trade stories about mutual friends, while Ms. Morrison had a cigarette, which, when she finished, she snuffed and put back into the pack with a knowing wink. "Taglocks," she said. "Never can be too careful," I replied. We are aware of the problems that can arise from leaving DNA from hair, saliva on a cigarette butt, or a used napkin accessible to others. Policing these items is one of the smartest things a magical practitioner can do.

That is one of my favorite parts of *Utterly Wicked:* not only does it stretch our ideas about curses (Hexing a lousy habit? Using a poppet to nurse yourself back to health?), but it helps us protect ourselves against hexes by knowing the methods employed to lay them. Don't leave your hairbrush with hair in it. Get your possessions back from exes, both friends and lovers. This book is recommended reading for everyone. It helps break curses and hexes, as well as lay them. It helps the reader learn to spot charlatans and provides the tools to combat fear, hatred, and malice. *Utterly Wicked* also supplies user guides for dirts (from the graveyard to the courthouse and everything in between), washes, powders, and more. Whether you like making healing waters or collecting dirt from various travels, or if you enjoy wandering cemeteries or want to dress an 11" fashion doll because you hate sewing, this book is for you.

Since I began practicing magic as a young lady, I like to feel I'll always look at it with fresh eyes. It was easy for people to dismiss my experiences at eighteen when I joined my first "adult" coven. That's how I knew my first high priestess wasn't the right fit. Every sentence she spoke to me sounded as if she were patting me on the head. The first person to treat me as a potential magician of worth was a Hoodoo practitioner, who said that I was starting to become who I was going to be, and that I had to act like it. Dorothy understands your worth, reader. She's here to show you how to step into being the practitioner you know you are going to be.

Remember, magic is agency. Magic is the ability to stand up for yourself when enough is enough. It is the voice in your gut that says, "You don't have to take this." Whether it's gossiping coworkers or a boss who thinks sexual harassment is a benefit of the position—you can change things for the better. Not only do you deserve to be protected and cherished, but you are making things better and safer for the ones who come after you. It may be scary or complicated, but I have faith in you, and so does Dorothy.

—Amy Blackthorn, owner of Blackthorn Hoodoo Blends, author of *Blackthorn's Botanical Magic* and *Sacred Smoke*

Acknowledgments

I have wonderful childhood memories of climbing into bed with my mother for a nightly bedtime story. It was always something exciting—filled with good guys and bad guys, and the choices that they made. Of course, the good guys always won. But not without severe hardship, difficult decision-making, and the gumption to stand up for themselves. And certainly not without the support of their friends.

Such was the case with this book. Obstacles appeared. Life got in the way. There were times that I wasn't even sure I'd get through it. But still, I kept going, stopping for directions when I lost my way, and asking for assistance when the going got rough. And it's to those folks who came to my aid that I owe a huge vote of thanks. I couldn't have done this without you!

To my husband, Mark—whom I love and adore more than words can say—for his undying support, for putting up with all those strange goings-on in our house, and for understanding the importance of SIPS and HIPS left burning on the altar.

To my dear friend, M. R. Sellars, for the role he played in getting me to write this book, for sharing poppet ideas (who'd have thought that grown men played with fashion dolls?), for countless hours of commiseration and brainstorming, and of course, for his delightful reaction to the *Curse of the Plastic Headband*. (Just so you know . . . my head's back to normal now!)

To Dameon Wilburn, Celeste Stone, Mary Caliendo, and Bick Thomas, for sharing magical ideas, personal recipes, curses, and hexes, for assisting in research, and just for being the wonderful folks they are.

To Christopher Penczak, for selflessly sharing his notes and thoughts on cursing tablets, and giving me insight into these interesting devices.

To Karl Madden, for coining the phrase, "Queen Bitch of the Whole F***ing Universe," and so generously sharing it with me.

To Z Harrell, for reminding me of the "oops factor," and for loving me just the way I am. (I'd be lost without you!)

To David Norris for graciously allowing the use of his poems in this book, and for applying personal ego boosts along the way, and to Kim Perkins-Murillo, for unwittingly supplying kicks in the ass when I needed them most.

To Sabrina the Ink Witch, my sister from another family, for generously allowing the use of her fabulous artwork for the cover, for doing more to promote this book than the law allows—well, almost!—and to Tina Hodges, who takes much better care of me than I deserve, even when being forced to accompany me to the jewelry store. (I love you both without measure!)

To Hoodoo Sen Moise, Christian Day, Nicki McDermott, and Mimi Lansou for their constant love and support—even when I'm at my worst—and more acts of kindness than I can count.

To Judika Illes, Editing Goddess Incarnate, who believed in this book, shared my vision, and went to great lengths to get it back on the market. (Thank you for being you!)

To Red Wheel/Weiser, who, by releasing this book, has proven itself to be one of the most gutsy and innovative publishers in the industry. I've never been more proud to be associated with a publishing house than I am with yours.

Finally, to everyone who's ever screwed me over and said there was nothing I could do about it: I just did. You gave me the impetus to write this book and for that, I thank you all from the bottom of my heart!

Introduction

Wicked Witches.

Evil sorcerers.

Things that go bump in the night.

Whether through fairytales, nursery rhymes, or the occasional movie, these become a part of our lives long before we can walk or talk. They shape our innermost fears, have the ability to cause cold sweats, and reduce us to little more than a pair of shaking knees. Even so, they form an important and productive part of who we are, for by their very introductions into our lives, they also force us to plant those first seeds of courage, fertilize them into worthwhile battle tools, and bring them to harvest with the need to stand up for ourselves, our rights, and our beliefs. They are the very things that make us capable of screaming "Bullshit!" at the tops of our lungs, and simply refusing to take the crap anymore.

Not that any of it's easy or quickly forthcoming. It takes time. So much time, in fact, that we usually ingest a lot of crap before refusing another helping. But eventually, we're done. We look at the plates in front of us—the ones still heaped with all of that ghastly mess—and consider our options. And with the garbage can overflowing and nowhere else to toss that stuff, with churning bellies already so full of it that the very thought of swallowing any more makes us gag, we push back our chairs and decide to take a stand.

Or not.

If the last two words apply to you, if you can bear the thought of being screwed over one more time, or if you think that every crisis in the world can be solved with love and goodwill, then take notice. I've written the next sentence just for you:

Close this book now and put it back on the shelf.

This is not a book for those who believe that life can be lived without ever harming anyone. This is not a book for those who are overly concerned with Karma, the Threefold Law, and the Golden Rule. Nor is it a book for the squeamish, the straightlaced, or the easily offended.

If you are any of these, I certainly wish you much luck on your path. But know that it would be in your best interest to take notice as well: Just refer to the italicized sentence above, and act in kind.

So, who precisely is this book for? It's for those folks who are sick and tired of swallowing the bullshit served up by other people. It's for those folks who are fighting mad and livid pissed. Yes, it's for those folks who are tired of taking a screwing at every turn, who are ready to wage war, and who have finally mustered the gumption to do something about it.

In short, it's for those folks who have what it takes to *become* the things that go bump in the night and aren't afraid to go there.

If you're that person, then read on. This is the book for you!

Although this book is subtitled *Hexes, Curses, and Other Unsavory Notions,* not everything you'll find within its pages is designed to do someone harm. Its contents are, instead, designed to help you to manipulate undesirable circumstances, remove problem areas, and recreate your life into something worth living again. And no matter how you try to convince yourself otherwise, you can't always do that without stepping on a few toes. You also need the right tools—tools, unfortunately, that folks neither want to talk about nor disclose—the very tools that I offer in this book.

For years, I went about the business of everyday living in much the same way as any number of other magical practitioners. I controlled my environment and my circumstances with a mixture of mundane action and magical assistance. I always looked for a solution that would benefit all involved. It worked and everyone was happy.

But then a series of events turned my life upside down. I tried everything in my magical repertoire, but nothing made the slightest bit of difference. I hit one brick wall after another as they collectively boxed me in and held me at bay. And that wonderful life I'd built? It suddenly seemed to take the proverbial form of quicksand, giving way beneath my feet and doing its damnedest to suck me under.

Now, hitting brick walls has a way of getting my attention, and it wasn't long before I realized that being nice simply wasn't going to cut it. I was going to have to handle my problems in the same fashion they'd been dished out, and toss them back on terms my opponents could understand. Yes . . . I was going to have to buck up, grow a backbone, soar right past ugly, and keep on going. In order to protect everything I held dear and make things right again, I was going to have to become that heart-pumping nightmare from which there is no return—the one guaranteed to make cold sweat pop wetly onto the brow of the Wicked Witch herself and reduce her to little more than a quivering heap. Plain and simple, I was going to have to instill enough fear so that nobody would even dream of messing with me or mine again, much less try it.

And that's precisely what I did.

Was it easy? Of course not. I talked to lots of people, did a ton of research and delved into some lesser-known areas that might make other folks cringe. There was also more experimentation than I even want to think about. But the hardest part of it all was changing my mind-set into something that would work toward the situation at hand rather than exacerbate it. At the end of it all, though, I found not only the exact tools necessary to solve my problem but also the courage to implement them without so much as batting an eyelash.

That said, I pass these tools along to you, the reader. It's my hope that you'll use them wisely and not without severe provocation. When in doubt, just remember this: Never use a sledgehammer on a fly when a simple swat with the proper device will do. It only makes a mess that someone will have to clean up later—and that someone is likely to be you!

Part One

The Morrigan stirs
The ancient broth.
Her finger tests it to her taste.
Sometimes bitter,
Sometimes sweet,
She is creator of the brew
And we dispense it by our hand
To scald or freeze
Depending on the appetite
Of those who wait.
You cannot work the ancient fire
Without the means to scorch.

David O. Norris, from "Calliach Fire"

Chapter One

A Hex Upon Thee

I like people. For the most part, they're a pleasant group who tend to cheer for the underdog, help their neighbors, and are unbelievably passionate about their beliefs. Add that to their individual quirks, eccentricities, and euphemisms, and they're more entertaining than any show on Broadway.

Especially when they feel threatened.

When fear is involved, the flight or fight factor comes into play. And because we've all been taught that fighting is tantamount to inappropriate behavior, the thought of walking away from any threatening situation will certainly cross our minds. But since an integral part of the human condition is survival—and survival can be defined on many levels—the fight option crosses our minds too. We weigh our options, check our limitations, and make a decision. And all we can hope for is that it's the right one.

The same is true for magical practitioners. But what really confuses me is that, even with all the resources at their disposal—resources that others can't even imagine—they'll usually take the flight route and call it good. Why? Well, it's a matter of personal belief systems. Some subscribe to the "harm none" sector of the Wiccan Rede. Others are concerned with the Threefold Law or the Laws of Karma. And with those in mind, they wouldn't even dream of doing anything magically that wasn't for the good of all. Regardless of the circumstances. Regardless of impending danger. Regardless of the personal harm that fleeing might bring to themselves or those they love.

If this line of thinking weren't so ridiculous, I might be amused. But it is. And I'm not.

Yes, I do subscribe to the version of the Wiccan Rede that says " . . . ever mind the law of three unless in self-defense it be . . . " But even if I didn't, I wouldn't feel any differently. That's because the "harm none" section is included in every version of the Rede known to Wicca. And if we truly subscribe to the rules in any of those texts, it's pretty clear that we shouldn't allow ourselves to be harmed either. We are, after all, part of that "none."

But what if we don't subscribe to the Rede? What if we live by the Threefold Law or the Laws of Karma instead? Well, I can promise you that neither of them is intended to set us up for serious damage, physical or otherwise. It's highly unlikely that anything nasty would come back to us simply because we were defending ourselves. But if it did? Well, I'm willing to take that risk. Are you?

Though the Rede, the Threefold Law, and the Laws of Karma may apply to most of us, it may not apply to all. It could be that some of us live by the Golden Rule. (You know the one. It's that rule that orders us to do unto others as we would have them do unto us.) Well, it doesn't hold water either. If I caused intentional harm to someone, I'd certainly expect for them to act in kind. Case closed.

Still not sure? Then consider this. If a serial killer were holding a gun to your head, a knife to your neck, or was delightedly slicing off bits of your flesh, would you be the least bit concerned about his well-being? Would you really give a rat's ass if he was happy? Secure in his own skin? That he would somehow manage to get out of the situation safely and without personal, physical, or psychological damage? Of course not! The rules would be damned, and all you'd care about would be getting away and seeing to it that he was too incapacitated to hurt you or anyone else ever again.

It's only a matter of common sense. And that's something we should also use when practicing magic.

Please understand that I'm not saying that we should never look for a peaceable solution or a solution that is good for everyone concerned. But there comes a time when none of that is going to work. And it's at that point that we have to decide whether to stand up for ourselves in the magical realm—or whether to just lie down and be beaten to a pulp.

It's never an easy decision. But fortunately, there's help in some simple rules of thumb:

1. If you wouldn't do it on the physical plane, don't do it in the magical realm. In short, make sure the measure of defense you employ fits the crime.

2. If it makes you uncomfortable, don't do it. Explore your options again, and look for a solution you can live with.

3. Be willing to own your actions and accept absolute responsibility for them.

See? That wasn't so hard. And once you incorporate those three little items into your life and make them your policy for everyday living, you won't have anything to worry about—magically, physically, or otherwise.

Fire in the Hole

Magic works. Of that I have no doubt. The same is true of every magical practitioner in the world; otherwise, they wouldn't even bother with the ancient arts. To do so would be absolutely pointless.

If that's so, though, how did anyone ever get the idea that curses only affect those who believe in them, and that those who don't are able to escape their grasp? Since this idea could've been spawned by any number of communications mediums—the internet, television, movies, or even some misguided author—it's hard to say. But there are two things I know for sure:

1) There are folks who actually believe this tripe, and 2) those who do have never been more wrong about anything in their lives.

Successful magic hinges solely on the belief of those people setting it into motion. If they believe in their abilities to effect the change they want, they can visualize it happening. That ability to watch it unfold in their minds' eyes gives them the impetus necessary to believe that the desired result will take place. And once that belief is in place, the magic takes flight, soars through the Cosmos, charts a direct path to its target, and—*WHAM!*—the intended desire manifests on the physical plane and becomes absolute reality. Magic truly is a matter of ". . . seeing is believing . . ."

That said, the end result has nothing at all to do with the recipient's mind-set. It doesn't matter whether he or she believes in its power. It doesn't matter whether he or she thinks the whole thing is a load of crap. Once loosed, the magic is going to hit its target. It is going to affect change. And there's not one damned thing the party on the receiving end can do about it.

True enough, there's something to be said for throwing up a shield to deflect the effort. But since I've never known a practitioner to give anybody a heads-up that magic is aimed in their direction—something they'd have to know in order to shield—that's probably a moot point. And if they're smart enough to have automatic shields in place? Well . . . the best they can hope for is to revise the effect somewhat and perhaps weaken its impact. Even the best of shields are not going to completely obliterate a spell already in progress. That's why we call it "magic."

This is especially true of curses, hexes, and other unsavory forms of magic. It's not that their actual ingredients are more powerful, though. It has, instead, to do with the emotion that fuels them: that raw, untamed emotion that goes way beyond peel-me-off-the-ceiling anger and can only be termed as livid pissed. And livid pissed is exactly what we are by the time we get around to even considering such things.

The old adage of adding fat to the fire doesn't even begin to cover it when fueling magic with this sort of emotion. In fact, it's more like adding a hefty dose of jet fuel to a hearth fire. There's going to be more than a minor flare-up. There's going to be an explosion to end all explosions. And anyone who thinks that a simple shield is going to deflect that sort of energy definitely has another think coming.

There's more. Just as any sort of explosion leaves a residue, so does this kind of energy. However, the residue left by a curse or hex is much more difficult to remove than that of its physical counterpart. Undetected, it flies like silt into emotional nooks and crannies, creeps into areas of the subconscious, and just generally messes with the recipient's mind. This makes the results not only life-changing but long-lasting. And, more than likely, that's the real reason this sort of magic wound up with the reputation for being stronger than any other.

To Curse or Not to Curse: That Is the Question

Over the course of your magical practice, this is a question that's eventually going to pop up. So, maybe some exploration is in order: Just exactly what warrants a curse and what doesn't?

The fact that Joe got the job you wanted probably doesn't warrant anything other than crossing off that place of employment and sending out resumes to the next ten on your list. And if you want to work a little magic to get one of those positions, so be it.

But what if the situation isn't that simple? What if the job in question was an inner company promotion, and you happen to know that Joe willfully sabotaged you? Maybe he took credit for some of your work—work that may have either qualified you for the position or caused the department head to take special notice of your application. Perhaps he even lied about you, saying that you were difficult to work with, that you weren't a team player, or that you had an attitude problem. Is that any reason to curse him?

Maybe. Maybe not. It just depends on the circumstances. And to come to a rational decision, you're going to have to look at the whole picture.

First, review the job description again, and really scrutinize the duties involved. If they're vague, Joe may have done you a favor, even if unwittingly. It might be that the job in question would take up more time than you're willing to give; time that would be best enjoyed somewhere else or even spent with your family. It could also be that the extra money involved is not worth what it's going to take to earn it. And if either is likely, then curses should be the furthest thing from your mind. In fact, you should probably think seriously about sending Joe a congratulatory gift.

But what if neither of those scenarios is true? What if Joe simply set out to ruin your reputation with the company—a company you've given your all to—and is now doing his dead level best to get you fired?

While none of that is good by any stretch of the imagination, I'm not sure such action truly deserves a curse either. Why? Because you definitely have other options. You could work magic to protect your job. You could work magic to shed light on Joe's behavior and show him to all concerned for the jackass that he really is. And if you're suddenly feeling magnanimous—which is doubtful at this point—you could even go so far as to work magic so that Joe finds a position more to his liking outside of the company. Any of those options will take care of the situation nicely—and without the need for a curse.

But now, let's change the scenario a bit. Let's say that you've been the victim of Joe's sexual harassment for a very long time and that the promotion was your ticket out of that mess. Let's say that when he found out you'd decided to apply for the job, he not only led you to believe that the problems with him would get much worse than you ever dreamed if you went through with it, but he also promised to ruin you with the company. That's not all. He also promised to personally squelch any chance of your getting alternative employment in the area. You've already seen how he works, so there's no doubt he can make good on all of this.

Now do you have good reason for a curse? You bet you do.

Of course, if you'd just turned Joe in to his superiors when he made his first lascivious move—if you'd decided to fight instead of flee back then—he wouldn't be in any position to bother you. In fact, he probably wouldn't even still be with the company. You could have avoided this whole mess, you might be sitting pretty in your new corner office, and there would be no reason for any sort of magic at all.

While playing the would've-should've-could've game is normally a complete waste of time, it definitely bears some thought here. For one thing, we need to learn from our mistakes. But perhaps more importantly, this sort of self-examination helps us to figure out what else is necessary to keep us from ever having to curse someone again. And it often takes some mighty deep digging to get to the root of the problem and yank it from our lives forever.

So, why didn't you report Joe's inappropriate behavior when he first got out of line? Chances are, you were afraid. But since precisely what you were afraid of holds the key here, that's what we need examine. Was it that you thought reporting him wouldn't solve the problem and that his superiors wouldn't take you seriously? Were you afraid that Joe would twist things around in such a way that you'd lose your job? Or were you simply afraid of that sick feeling that makes your stomach churn every time you're faced with confrontation?

Since such is usually the case when folks won't stand up for themselves, I'm betting on the latter. And for all practical purposes, let's say I'm right. What you need now—before you even think of performing that curse—is something to keep you from ever being in that position again. You need some gumption. And the best way I know of getting some is to perform the spell below.

The Gimme Gumption Spell

Materials:

> *1 reversible candle, black on white (Alternatively, color a white candle completely with a black permanent marker.)*
> *1 shot glass filled with rum, bourbon, scotch, or vodka (Substitute a shot glass of water flavored with rum extract, if you like.)*

Since this is a war of sorts—and Mars energy is essential for any type of successful battle—plan to perform this spell on a Tuesday on either the Full or New Moon. Fill the glass and light the candle, then place the glass directly in front of you. Ground and center in your normal fashion, then say something like:

> *Confrontation is not my foe,*
> *It's not an opponent; it causes no woe.*

It is my friend now and, as such,
It straightens out the cause of much
Confused and wrongful accusation,
Misunderstanding, and misinformation.
It smoothes out wrinkles while it mends
Relationships that might otherwise end.
It no longer makes me sick,
For now I've finally learned the trick:
That anger plays no part; instead,
Resolution weaves its threads.
That said, I now infuse with gutsy gumption
This liquid for my own consumption.

At this point, think about what gumption and courage mean to you, then hold the glass aloft, and blow that thought across the liquid to infuse and charge it. Place the glass in front of the candle and continue, saying something like:

And before this candle, it is placed,
So its energies will interlace
With my infusion to bring it power
As it burns by minute and by hour,
To banish worries, woes, and fears,
To banish nervous shakes and tears,
And brings forth the courage that I need
To defend myself with grace and speed.
The gumption asked for now is won,
As I will, so be it done.

When the candle extinguishes itself, drink the liquid, feel the courage flow through your body, and make a firm resolve never to be stomped on again.

Do You Have What It Takes?

Curses are not for the namby-pamby. Nor are they for fluffy bunnies or for those who insist that even the worst of horrors happen for a reason. They are for gutsy folks with the courage to do something about their situations when all other possibilities have been exhausted.

But just the same, curses aren't to be taken lightly or flung about without due cause and serious thought. They're not your normal type of magic and certainly not anything that should be performed as readily as a protection spell or a money spell. In fact, there's good reason that they're usually at the top of the magical practitioner's ten-foot-pole list. And contrary to popular belief, taking responsibility for your actions is the least of your worries.

To start with, cursing someone takes an inordinate amount of energy. Your energy. Energy that you've stored for other things, like the simple business of everyday living. And cursing someone effectively is going to wipe out all your reserves. But even if that weren't the case, it's important to remember that you're going to be transferring that energy to the person on the other end of your magic. So, there's a good chance that you're inadvertently going to pick up some of that person's energy along the way too. Do you really want that nasty stuff on you? Probably not.

Another thing is that the only substance that will fuel a curse properly is anger. Trying to fuel it with love or adding a "for the good of all concerned" codicil simply isn't going to cut it. In order to even get the spell off the ground, you're going to have to be so mad that you can't see straight. So mad that even strangling the person in question with your bare hands wouldn't be enough to suit you. Yes, you're going to have to be absolutely, uncontrollably, beyond the shadow of a doubt, livid pissed—more infuriated and enraged than you've ever been in your entire life and are ever likely to be again. And you need to know whether you've got what it takes to work yourself up into that sort of irrepressible hissy fit. What's more, though, do you even want to?

Further, you're also going to have to believe that you are unquestionably correct in the need to curse someone. Rationalization to suit your own purposes isn't going to get it. You have to be right. You have to be sure. There isn't any room for error or an after-the-fact "Oops . . . I was mistaken" when it comes to curses. The effects can be finite. What's more, you can't even begin to second-guess yourself. Do you have that sort of resolve?

If none of this bothers you, and you're absolutely certain of your position, then a curse is probably the way to go. And if not? Well, it's best left alone.

Is It a Hex—or Is It Memorex?

We already know that a good many magical practitioners normally won't even entertain the idea of hexing someone—not even if they're scared witless—but there is one thing that will cause them to consider the idea. Simply put, it's the notion that someone else has had the balls to toss one of those ghastly concoctions in their direction. It's a simple matter of fighting fire with fire and engaging their opponent in terms they'll understand. Even so, this conclusion only comes after so many failed attempts to alleviate the problem peaceably that they're blue in the face from exhaustion.

If you are one of these people and that's why you're reading this book, read on. This section is for you.

Before you go too far with this, take a good hard look at the facts. Think about why the possibility of a curse didn't occur to you at the onset of your difficulties. Recount the related problems you've experienced to the present, and try to pinpoint the time they began. (It helps to make a list.) Then look for any semblance of reason for their occurrence.

Once you've finished, give some serious thought to what led you to change your mind and come to the conclusion that a hex had been tossed your way. List the events in chronological order, and again, look for reasonable explanations. Jot down any that pop up.

So, why am I having you do all this? Because if you can find plausible reasons for any of the personal trials and tribulations connected to the time period, it could be that a curse may not be the culprit at all—or in any event, not one delivered at the hands of someone else. It's quite possible that you, yourself, are at fault. And if that's the case, the last thing you want to do is activate a curse.

Fact of the matter is that we are often our own worst enemies. We constantly set ourselves up for disaster in any number of ways. Sometimes, it's a matter of giving folks too much personal information. Sometimes, it's a matter of being ill-prepared or less than diligent about dealing with details. But most of the time it's a matter of procrastinating or—although it's true, I really hate to say this—being too lazy to handle our tasks efficiently. We just expect things to handle themselves, and they don't. But unfortunately, this sort of behavior is a part of the human condition.

Depression can also play a large role in things going awry in our personal lives. It breeds a moldy sort of negativity that stifles the creative flow. And once that flow ebbs to the point of just barely eking out, the good things in our lives seem to follow suit. That's when we begin to feel sorry for ourselves and plop right down on the pity pot. It's not a fun place to sit, but we do it anyway, just watching as the world passes us by and everything in our lives goes to hell in a hand basket.

One of the biggest culprits of self-sabotage, however, is confusing entitlement with self-empowerment—and the two aren't even remotely synonymous. Self-empowerment is finding the motivation to live life on our own terms, acting upon that motivation, and accepting the responsibility for doing so. Entitlement, on the other hand, is to believe that life owes us something and that we can do anything we please without the slightest regard to the consequences. There's a big difference.

The problem is that those who have entitlement issues are eventually rudely awakened. And that rude awakening is generally administered on both the mundane and spiritual planes. These folks soon discover that people simply will not put up with their shit. Neither will they put up with the accompanying arrogance nor the complete disregard for how their actions affect the rest of humankind. No one wants to be around them, and they eventually find themselves ostracized to the point of having no moral support system at all.

Then the spiritual realm gets in on the act. The powers that be knock them around a few times to get their attention. And if they don't take immediate notice and cut the crap, stronger measures become necessary. Things get worse and worse until the spiritual support system disappears as well. Nothing works. They hit one brick wall after another. And yet, they still don't get it. Even with so much negative stuff going on, it never occurs to them that they are even remotely at fault. No siree, Bob. Instead, it must be someone else's doing. Someone must have put a curse on them.

When that notion enters their heads, the really fun stuff begins. Acting just like some sort of psychic magnet, that single thought travels through the mind collecting others. Together, they roll along gathering momentum, gathering speed, and gathering density, until finally—bigger than life and twice as ugly—this nasty ball of crap crashes right through the forbidden gate and unleashes paranoia. And once that's loosed upon the mind and given free rein, pinpointing who might have initially tossed out a hex or why is no longer an issue. Why? Because now they've convinced themselves that there's not just one person involved; instead, everybody on the planet is out to get them. Their lives are completely and irrevocably ruined, and nothing—not even death itself—is ever going to fix it.

It's a curse, all right, but it's self-made, self-directed, and self-inflicted. And fighting fire with fire just isn't a good idea in this case. It's tantamount to blowing themselves up. And they'd come out far less damaged if they just pulled the pin on a hand grenade and swallowed it.

So, do yourself a favor. Stay calm, stay collected, and make that list I've described above. You'll be able to make a reasonable decision about what to do next. And best of all, paranoia can stay sealed in that airtight cage, precisely where it belongs.

A Hex by Any Other Name

There are probably as many different types of hexes and curses as there are magical practitioners. Some call for multiple ingredients and a good amount of planning. Others call for a gesture of the hand, the face, or other body part. Still others don't require anything but the spoken word. But even with something as simple as that, the delivery of those words seems to vary from shouted, muttered, or coldly whispered. And with each practitioner insisting that his or her curse is the very best ever concocted, trying to choose is enough to make your head spin.

So, how do you decide which sort to use? And once you do, how do you know that your choice is the right one for the job?

First, don't let it overwhelm you. Just search for one that suits both your purpose and your lifestyle. Or better yet, construct your own. If you're not sure where to start, take a look at which Element rules your astrological sign. I've discovered that personal magical power is often strongest when it involves that Element— Earth signs tend to bury things, Fire signs tend to burn things, and so on—and your comfort levels will reap the benefits as well.

Second, don't bother with an obscure ingredient list. (You're not going to find an authentic hand of glory—not even on the internet—and constructing your own is going to land you right in the pokey!) Either find a reasonable substitution or do a little more research.

In the meantime, though, it may help to know a little about the systems and cultures from where most curses and hexes are derived. And to that end, brief descriptions of the most common follow below.

Hoodoo? You Do!

A good number of these sorts of spells come from a popular magical system called Hoodoo. This is in no way, shape, or form a religious system—it's magic, plain and simple—and its origin is attributed to derivations of the magical practices of the Afro-Caribbean people who were once enslaved in the United States.

One of the reasons for the popularity of this system is that nothing is hard and fast. Ingredients are easy to find, and substitutions can be made with ease. That's because, unlike most other magical systems, precisely how hoodoo is practiced varies greatly according to specific agricultural region and available resources. This means that although there may be a few common threads, you're not likely to find the same sort of practices in Louisiana as you would in South Carolina, in Georgia as you would in Texas, and so on. And this probably has to do with the fact that the enslaved were literally scattered all across the country and simply used what was handy to work their magic. As a result, hoodoo truly is folk magic at its best.

Before we get too far, though, there's something that I'd like to make crystal clear: Hoodoo magic is not necessarily dark. It's just more honest than most other types of practice, and so are the folks who practice it. If they're going to throw down with a hex, they don't bother to disguise it with some other sort of magic. They just do it, make no bones about it, and go on about their business.

With that out of the way, magical efforts within the system aren't called spells. They're called tricks, a classification that's steeped in honesty too. A spell, after all, is a manipulation of the Elements to get what you want. And stripped right down to the bare bones, what exactly is manipulation? Simply put, it's tricking someone—or something—into doing your bidding.

The other difference between hoodoo and other systems is that magical efforts aren't charged. But lest you get the wrong idea, that doesn't mean that tons of energy isn't placed within their folds. Nothing could be further from the truth. Because tricks usually take the form of packets or parcels—their contents are usually wrapped up in something or contained in a bag—they are "laid." This means that, once completed, the parcels are placed somewhere out of view. And whether laid in the ground, under a porch, or in the water, that's what completes their magic.

As an aside, it's interesting to note that tricks are seldom as easily broken as spells. It's not that the magic involved is any stronger. It's that breaking a trick involves locating the parcel, dismantling it, and destroying the contents. This presents a whole new set of problems: finding the hiding place and finding the trick, both of which can be a real effort in futility. But even if you manage to find both, that still may not be enough to uncross the victim. Depending upon method of disposal and mediums used for contents and wrapping, a good portion of the trick may have rotted away or dissolved. The tiny fragment you've got left may not be able to handle the job—at least, not with any measure of success. And this is probably how hoodoo got its current reputation: that of absolute power and darkness.

Whose Curse Is Worse?

Contrary to what some folks may think, the Afro-Caribbean people and their descendants neither single-handedly hold the monopoly on great curses, nor did they invent the pin-struck poppet for which they are so famous. The roots of the poppet, in fact, go all the way back to the ancient Egyptians. Instead of being made of cloth, wood, and plant materials, though, the figure was cast of wax and designed to closely resemble the subject in question. How, precisely, they came up with using wax is anyone's guess, but the implications certainly speak for themselves. It was easily poked with pins to cause pain, bent and distorted to damage the body, and of course, melted away to cause a slow and painful death.

But that wasn't the only form by which the Egyptians exacted revenge. They also understood that the power of words lived on long after the scribe who wrote them or the person who uttered them. And although no actual artifact or photograph exists as proof, it's been said that such a curse, inscribed on clay tablets found in the antechamber of Tutankhamen's tomb, was responsible for the many deaths surrounding its excavation. So, what did this supposed inscription say?

"Death will slay with its wings whoever disturbs the peace of the pharaoh."

And whether any such inscription truly existed or not, it appears that Death took notice anyway and did just that.

Then, there were the ancient Romans and Greeks. And as one might expect from people who went to so much trouble to perfect a vast array of protection talismans, they also had their hands in the cauldron of torment—and all the way up to their elbows. Their curses involved tablets made of metal, though, which were inscribed with instructions to the Gods of the Underworld before depositing them in a place appropriate to the intention. As an extra boon, metals sacred to specific underworld Deities were often used to entice Them to lend Their services.

Lead was an extremely popular medium for several reasons. And while I feel sure that its associations with Saturn, the underworld, and revenge were definitely considerations, the fact that it was easily obtainable, inexpensive, long lasting, and easy to carve must have also figured heavily into the choice. And while it's doubtful that the ancient Greeks and Romans actually knew that lead was toxic, I can't think of any better medium upon which to craft a curse than on something inherently poisonous. Can you?

The intentions of these curse tablets covered much the same sorts of subject matter that interest us today: litigation, justice, business, competition, and matters of the heart. But the manners in which they were delivered to the Gods of the Underworld? Interesting, to say the least. While occasionally buried on the property of the person targeted, the location of a sporting competition, or the courthouse, they were most often tossed into pools of stagnant water (the equivalent of today's sewers) or buried in the right hand of a corpse to gain its assistance. (The underlying thought with employing the latter was that the corpse would be really annoyed at having been disturbed, see the name on the tablet, and not only carry out the torment listed, but add a bit of its own!)

The ancient Celts had their own system of curse delivery as well. While they were almost always spoken—or at least, accompanied by an incantation spoken in verse—there was something else that set their system apart from the others. You see, they believed that to curse someone took extreme amounts of concentration. So to that end, they often employed some measure of physical difficulty—standing on one foot with one eye closed, or perhaps, pointing at the victim—during delivery as a way of keeping their minds on their business. Of course, I'm sure that this also scared the hell out of their victims. And instilling that sort of fear is bound to have produced a double whammy.

That brings us to the Italian practitioners. While most of us associate them solely with the use of malocchio or the evil eye, the strength of their curses is much more involved than that. Instead, it lies in subtle gesture and action—in the stirring of a soup, in the washing of the hands, and today, perhaps, even in the shredding of an email. But that's not all. They also have a knack for incorporating the most innocuous of objects. (Who, after all, would have ever imagined that all those dreadful nightmares—the ones that make you afraid to even close your eyes at night—would be coming directly from your favorite pillow?) Some of the best Italian curses I've ever witnessed, in fact, were so cleverly placed that no one even saw them coming. And it's that sort of sly delivery that makes them so very powerful.

As an aside, I'd be negligent if I failed to point out that the early Christians—most specifically, those who authored the Bible—were no strangers to the world of curses, either. And according to them God Himself, tossed out the very first when He expelled a legion of angels from heaven and cast them into a fiery pit of His own creation. After that, though, it seems that He really got the hang of it. When He evicted Adam and Eve and their buddy, the snake, from the Garden of Eden, for example, other side effects were added. The menstrual period and the labor pains of childbirth were born, as was the dogma of original sin and the purgatory that went with it. And that was just the beginning. Cain was cursed for killing Abel, the Babylonians were cursed for building the Tower of Babel, Lot's wife was cursed and turned to salt, the world was cursed and destroyed by flood, and on and on and on. So even if the early Christians weren't actually adept at flinging curses themselves, their God sure was. And because of that, it's no surprise that many of today's curses come directly from and/or utilize passages in the Bible.

Of course, there are literally hundreds of other magical systems that employ the use of hexes, curses, and other unsavory notions, but there's simply not space here to go into all of them. So, do a bit of research. Borrow ideas. And incorporate those newly discovered tidbits into spells and rituals of your own. That is, after all, what truly powerful magic is all about.

Chapter 2

The Real Dirt on the Quick and the Dead

No one who's ever read *Midnight in the Garden of Good and Evil*—or seen the movie by the same name—could ever forget the scenes where Minerva, the common-law wife of Dr. Buzzard, sits by his grave, spitting liquor and digging up dirt. His purple glasses perched on her nose, she gives Buzzard hell for not providing her with the right lottery numbers, while stabbing his grave so forcefully with a trowel that she might be trying to kill him if he weren't already dead.

It never fails to make me laugh out loud. But not for the reasons you might think. What really tickles me is that Minerva isn't like most folks who visit cemeteries. She's loud and sassy and pulls no punches. She wants Buzzard to know how she feels and to hear exactly what she has to say. And that makes Minerva real.

It's sad to think that most of us aren't real—at least, not when it comes to cemetery visits. We behave as if we're in church, in the library, or some other place where any volume over that of a whisper won't be tolerated.

What's Up with That?

Fact of the matter is that we're there to visit with the dead: to chat with them, to express ourselves, and maybe even to get a few answers. Problem is, though, we get caught up in the reverence factor. We assume that our dearly departed will see our quiet, unobtrusive demeanor as a sign of respect. And we have to be respectful of the dead, right? Otherwise, something awful is sure to happen.

Well, it might. But the worst that's likely to happen is that the whole visit will be in vain—that the dead might not hear us or even know we were there.

At this point, I can almost see you rolling your eyes heavenward and looking at this page aghast. I can almost hear you muttering too. But in between all that, your mind is probably going ninety-to-nothing, working desperately to call up a distant memory whose source you can't quite place. You know the one. It's that the dead can hear everything, even our innermost thoughts.

For those of you following this train of thought, I have three words: Stop right there.

To start with, we have no way of knowing what the spirits of the dead can hear and what they can't. But I'll tell you one thing for sure. They are certainly not Gods. And because of that, it only stands to reason that they can't hear anything that's left unspoken.

But what about this respect thing? Isn't that important? You bet it is. However, it's my opinion that the dead should be treated with the same amount of respect as the living. And that means going back to the most basic of good conversational manners. Simply put, it's rude to whisper. If you're going to say something, say it loudly enough for everyone to hear. And if you'd just as soon that everyone not hear? Then it's best to keep it to yourself.

All I'm saying is that it's okay to enjoy your cemetery visits. It's okay to be yourself. Just laugh and talk and have a good time. Make it the same sort of visit you'd have had with these folks if they were still alive. The dead can't help but enjoy a visit like that. What's more, they'll be looking more forward to your next one than you ever thought possible. And that's what it's all about, isn't it?

An Audience with the Queen

I was grown before I ever got the real scoop on cemeteries. I had no idea that they comprised the kingdom of a specific deity or that I needed Her permission to enter. I just went about my merry way, chatting with the spirits of those I loved, planting flowers, bringing presents, and doing what I did best: being my happy-go-lucky, sassy self.

Of course, I wasn't working magic on the grounds at the time and certainly wasn't gathering components for any sort of related effort. Had I been, the proper protocol would have been extremely important and, not followed carefully, may have brought about some undesired results. That said, there are a few things you should know before heading for a cemetery with magic in mind.

Most important, perhaps, is that Oya is the Queen of the Dead and holds domain over all cemeteries. (She's also in charge of commerce, so it's always propitious to stay on Her good side!) Don't let Her title fool you, though. She's a fun-loving sort with a real sense of humor. And once you get to know Her, you can't help but fall in love. She's just that sort of Goddess.

However, it is important to gain Her permission before entering Her kingdom, and here's where things can get sticky. It's been my experience that Oya does things when She feels like it, instead of on demand. She's been known to keep folks waiting at the gate for lengthy periods of time just to see what they'll do. And just about the time they've given up entirely and turn to leave, she unsettles them with a cackle loud enough to send them leaping into the air—what else would a queen without a court jester do for fun?—and allows them entrance. It's the funniest thing you've ever seen, provided it's happening to someone else.

There are a couple of things you can do to keep yourself from being on the receiving end of Oya's antics, so keep them in mind if you don't have time to wait around all day. First, cover your head with something white in Her honor. Ladies should wear a white scarf or lace mantilla, while men can wear a white ball cap. (Oya's all about good manners, though, so don't forget to remove your cap when gaining entrance, guys!)

Secondly, always bring Her some sort of enticement. She absolutely adores presents—I've never known Her to turn one down—and is especially partial to red wine and copper. (While either will do, I've found that offering Her both really speeds things up. Just put nine pennies in an old prescription bottle, add a few drops of red wine, and give it a good shake.) And above all, be sure to tell Oya that you've brought Her something when you first ask permission to enter. It will make all the difference in the world, in both Her attitude and your time.

Talking to Oya is easy. It's just a matter of talking to Her like you would anyone else. But since She definitely likes to be entertained, I've provided a brief request incantation you can use in Her honor. It's always worked for me, and I have no doubt that it will work for you as well.

Cemetery Entrance Incantation

Oh, Oya, I call on You! Please lift Your head
And grant me swift entrance, Oh Queen of the Dead,
Into Your kingdom. I've brought You a present—
Nine pennies in red wine—which I think You'll find
*   pleasant.*
I beg of You earnestly, grant me admission;
Let me enter Your realm without terms or condition!

Once you've gotten Oya's permission, enter the cemetery, uncap the bottle, and prepare to give Her the gift. But because protocol is important here, the pennies need to jingle together and make noise. The reason is that you're doing more right now than just giving Oya a present. You're also alerting the dead that they have company—it's a little like knocking on a door—and you want them to hear you. So, drop the wine-soaked pennies in the nearest urn or vase, on a plot curb, or in the paved or gravel pathway. If none of those options are available, not to worry. Just dump the coins into your hand, jingle them together, and toss them in front of you. Then go on about your business.

While you certainly don't require Oya's permission to leave the cemetery—you can go anytime you want—it's important to note that there's also a proper way to exit. Once you've finished thanking Oya and Her subjects for their time and for sharing their home with you, be sure to back out of the entrance. There are a couple of theories on why this is important. One school of thought is that the dead are tricksters and that only fools would turn their backs to them. But I think the one that makes more sense really has to do with good manners. Simply put, it's downright rude to turn your back to anyone. And you certainly don't want to insult the dead—especially if you want them to help you!

Digging Up Dirt

Contrary to popular belief, graveyard dirt isn't just used to cause someone harm. It can be a wonderful addition to all sorts of magic, especially when you want to pack a real wallop. And that's the reason that it's often used in curses.

I've always been told that you should obtain this dirt from the grave of one of your ancestors—someone whose blood runs through your veins—since you have an inherent connection to them, and their spirits should be more than willing to help you. It's a good point and one that I took to heart when I needed to obtain some graveyard dirt to resolve a particularly difficult situation. The problem was that I lived a thousand miles away from my parents' graves. And to compound matters, the only person who lived in close proximity to their gravesites not only wasn't a practitioner but would have felt like she was desecrating their graves if I'd asked her to help.

After giving the matter some serious thought, I finally decided on the next best thing. I'd just go out to a local cemetery, form a relationship with one of the spirits there, and then request dirt from his or her site. So to that end, I asked my husband the location of the nearest cemetery.

Now even though my husband isn't a practitioner, he's a much more powerful Witch than I'll ever hope to be. He always seems to know things that he couldn't possibly know and never fails to deliver whatever information I need just when I need it. This was one of those times.

"Well," he said, peering at me from over his newspaper, "if you really want *old* dirt, maybe you should just go out to Ball's Bluff."

To be perfectly honest, the age of the dirt hadn't even entered my mind. But he was definitely right on target on several levels. For one thing, Ball's Bluff is a Confederate battleground less than fifteen minutes away, and because I'm from the South with ancestors who fought for the Confederacy, it certainly fit the bill. But the age of the dirt was important too. My intention was to make someone leave me alone. And after the fact, I discovered that the oldest graveyard dirt you can find is precisely what's necessary to accomplish that successfully. So armed with a plastic bag and an old soup spoon, I headed in that direction.

When I arrived at Ball's Bluff, though, I was somewhat confused. Oh, I knew where the cemetery was, all right. That wasn't the problem. It's just that I'd expected to have a choice of spirits to chat with. But such was not the case, for the only Confederate soldier buried on the whole property—a property which covered acres and acres—was a brave young flag bearer by the name of Sergeant T. Clinton Hatcher. That being the case, I wasted no time in introducing myself to Sergeant Hatcher and striking up a conversation. I explained that I was a true child of the South, who my ancestors were, and how they were connected to him by cause. Then I explained that I needed the dirt from his grave to defend my name, to defend my honor, and to defend my very life.

I was more than prepared to wait for an answer. I was even prepared for no answer at all and the possibility of having to go to another cemetery. But what I wasn't prepared for was an affirmative answer so quick and so loud that it nearly scared me right out of my skin!

Once I regained my composure, I went to the center of the grave and began to dig. And that's when things got interesting. I heard a distinct "Not there, ma'am. Come closer. Up by the headstone."

I looked up to see who'd caught me in the act, since that's the sort of thing that usually happens to me, but there wasn't a soul in sight. It was then that I understood that Sergeant Hatcher's spirit was not only willing to help me but was guiding me as well. It was a damned good thing too, for no sooner had I gotten what I needed and buried the offering coins, several people strolled toward the cemetery. And had I not been immediately directed to the headstone where the ground was softer, I probably would've had to explain myself to those folks. Can you imagine?!

But the interesting part didn't end there. After I got back home, I decided to do a little research on the uses of graveyard dirt. And that's when I realized two very important things: That dirt should always be gathered from just below the headstone to make someone go away and, of course, that I owed Sergeant Hatcher big time. He'd not only managed to protect me from delivering an unbelievable explanation and possible jail time but had known exactly what he was talking about.

Of course, the full impact of the magic I'd been party to didn't actually hit me until I ran an internet search on my new friend, the sergeant. It was there that I found copies of some letters he'd written while in the army—letters to a woman with whom he'd fallen in love. That's when I knew for certain that I'd been drawn to his grave intentionally and that no other graveyard dirt I could have possibly gleaned from the area would have handled the job at hand. For there, within the letters written by this bright, amusing young man, I found my confirmation: Clinton Hatcher's pet peeve was men who were too cowardly to defend their women. Defense was exactly what I'd asked of him. And defense was exactly what I'd gotten.

There are probably as many theories on how to gather graveyard dirt as there are graves on the planet. And the truth of the matter is that the exact procedure just depends upon who you ask. For that reason, you'll only find my personal protocol listed in the guidelines below.

Timing: It's said that for good works, graveyard dirt should be taken within the hour before midnight and, for evil, within the hour after midnight. That's all well and fine, but it can really pose a problem in today's world. The reason is that most cemeteries are locked up tighter than a drum at dusk. And unless you want to open yourself up to a trespassing charge— and Gods know what else—you'd best be gathering your dirt during normal "business hours."

That said, I usually don't worry about what time of day I'm handling my collection. Instead, I simply tell the spirit precisely why I want the dirt and wait for permission. Yes, sometimes permission is denied, but that's okay too. When that happens, I just finish my conversation, thank the spirit for chatting with me, and strike up a conversation with another of the resident dead.

The only exception is when I need to work at cross-purposes with someone else. And for that, I begin my digging at times when the hands of the clock are in direct opposition to each other and in a position to cross-quarter its face if there were four hands instead of two. The exact times are 9:15, 12:30, 2:45, and 6:00.

Protection: Because spirits are not always the peaceable, gentle creatures we assume they are, you'll occasionally run across one who decides to wreak havoc with your work. For this reason I always wear a necklace that I've charged for protection when I enter a cemetery—any sort of amulet or talisman will do if it's charged properly—and then ask Oya for Her blessing. This keeps any ornery spirits at bay since not even the most mischievous would dare to mess with Her!

Payment: Never enter a cemetery without at least nine dimes in your pocket. There are several reasons for this. For one thing, it's polite to give something back in payment for the dirt you're taking, and nine dimes is the acceptable payment. There's also a theory that dimes cut the connection with harmful spirits, and if the dirt's paid for in that medium, they won't attach themselves to you or your property. In any case, I always bury the dimes where I've taken the dirt, and I've never had the slightest bit of trouble.

One more thing about the dimes: Some folks insist that only Mercury dimes be used for payment, as His likeness appears on the coins and entices Him to aid in communications. While I certainly see the sense in this, these particular dimes are not easy to come by anymore. So, if you want Mercury's help, a better solution might be to just come right out and ask Him for it.

Tools: While the most acceptable form of gathering dirt is to dig it with your hands, there's little I abhor more than getting dirt under my nails—and there's no way to dig by hand and keep that from happening. As a result, I've taken to using an old soup spoon. It's handy, it fits right in my purse, and it's easily cleaned between diggings with a baby wipe.

Some practitioners also like to use a knife for digging, as they say it cuts any connection to unsavory spirits that may be hanging around.

Storing: Some folks say it's unlucky to bring graveyard dirt into your home, but I've never found that to be true. However, I do keep it sealed in zippered plastic bags, labeled with my intention, the name of its donor, and the related birth and death dates.

Why even worry about the age of the donor? Because depending on the work at hand, age may actually have a bearing on the results—especially if you intend for the related spirit to aid you in your efforts. The dirt from a child's grave, for example, might work well for cementing a loving friendship but wouldn't do much good if a scorching melt-you-into-a-puddle romance was at stake. The rule of thumb here is to never use dirt from a donor who could not possibly have experienced your desired result. And proper labeling is one way of avoiding that pitfall.

One more thing. Please remember to check for earthworms before you bag the dirt, and release any that you find. I can't say for sure that dead earthworms are unlucky, but there's certainly no point in finding out!

Dealing with Spirits

While we've touched on the subject of gaining a spirit's permission to obtain and use dirt from its grave, this is something that truly bears further discussion—especially if you want the spirit in question to help you to achieve the desired result. Taking graveyard dirt without permission is much like breaking into someone's home and stealing their possessions. And if you did that on the physical plane, the only help you'd get from the injured party would be a one-way trip to jail.

The same is true of the spiritual realm. Yeah, I know that spirits don't necessarily live in the dirt in the cemetery. However, that dirt comprises the final resting place of the body it left behind. That means that its energy is in that dirt. And to take that without permission is to take the only possession it has left. Go that route and one thing's for sure: jail time is going to be the least of your worries.

You also need to remember that asking permission is not enough. Some sort of relationship must be formed with the spirit before proceeding. And depending upon the spirit and your individual needs, this could take a few minutes or several days. You also need to be prepared for the possibility that you're not going to be able to form a relationship at all. The reasons for this are many—personality clash, little or no common ground, or an objection to your desires, just to name a few—but in this case, none of that really matters. What does matter is that you don't push the issue. Just thank the spirit for its time, and continue with your search.

Once you do find a spirit that's willing to help you (and you will), payment for the dirt is not enough. Mind your manners, be polite, and thank it for its assistance. Bring it an extra token of appreciation. You never know when you might need its help again, and no one—living, dead, or otherwise—is going to be willing to offer support of any kind if you can't even be bothered with common courtesy.

Of course, if a spirit really likes you—if you've been kind and courteous and gone the extra mile—it may decide to hang around with you, whether you want it to or not. To avoid this, offer it a piece of black onyx as a parting gift once your goal is achieved. (It's the stone of separation and will sever your connections peaceably.) And if you need the spirit's assistance again? Not a problem. Just go back to visit, and be assured that it will remember you.

Getting Down to the Nitty Gritty

The old woman rubbed the back of her neck and stretched in her chair, then cast her eyes back toward the assortment of stones and bones in front of her. After studying them for a couple of seconds, she pushed her glasses back up to the bridge of her nose and looked at me directly. "You want that magic to work, baby?"

"Of course, I do," I countered. "Otherwise, I wouldn't even be considering it."

"Well," she said matter of factly, "you're gonna have to get dirt from an open grave. You're gonna have to . . . "

"An open grave?!" I screeched. "I'm not going to do that. I wouldn't even dream of going there. I . . . "

"Uh-hunh." She eyed me with such disgust that I wished I could disappear into thin air. I knew she thought I was nothing but a wuss and that the very idea made my blood run cold. She was right on both counts. But not for the reasons she imagined.

I leaned right into her personal space bubble, lifted my chin, and looked right into her eyes. "I don't care what you think," I said with equal disgust. "I know perfectly well what'll happen if I try something like that. There I'll be on my hands and knees, leaning over that grave, when suddenly, without any provocation whatsoever, I'll lose my balance and fall. And nothing—not love nor magic nor the Gods, Themselves—can make me put myself in that position."

"Figured as much," she said with a shrug, her voice softening, "but ain't nothin' stronger. Ain't nothin' gonna do the job any quicker. Ain't nothin' . . . "

"That may be. But I won't do it. I'll never claw my way out of that hole if I fall. I'll never . . . "

A wave of her hand stopped me in mid-sentence. "'Course you can always get dirt from the murdered or hanged and hope for the best, but if I was you, baby, I'd . . . " Her voice trailed off, and she turned her attention back to the objects in front of her.

"You'd what?"

"Nothin', baby. Nothin' at all. I'm just sayin' it's the best there is. No matter what it is that's ailin' you."

What sort of dirt you gather—and from which graves or establishments you gather it—depends solely on your intention and what you're comfortable with. Suffice it to say that I've never gleaned dirt from an open grave, no matter how strong it was or who thought I should. For one thing, I'm still way too clumsy for that sort of operation. And I'm not quite ready for that intimate of a relationship with the resident dead.

For another, though, unless you're dealing with a privately owned family cemetery, there simply isn't time to gather the dirt in question. Interment begins about twenty minutes after the service or just as soon as everybody's been shooed from the property, with fill-in commencing immediately after. So, unless you're related to the deceased—and don't care what the rest of your family thinks as you pull back the funeral carpet and reach under the casket with your baggie—it's a little more difficult to obtain this sort of dirt now than it was in years past.

Still, I'm not discounting its power. The old woman who first suggested I use it had years of experience in the field. And if I hadn't been so worried back then that I'd slip and fall into that hole myself, I might be able to give you a firsthand accounting. What I can tell you, though, is this. She was absolutely right about dirt taken from the murdered and executed. It's very powerful stuff. And I've never had it fail me. The same is true of old dirt, and when seeking a collection source, I find that the older the grave is, the better.

But what about dirt from other graves? Does it work well too? Absolutely! And for your convenience, a brief listing of the types I've found helpful and the purposes for which I think they're most useful follows below. Please note that this list is not in any way complete and is meant to be used as a guideline only. As you work with graveyard dirt, follow your own instincts, and you can't go wrong.

Adolescent (ages 11–19): Dirt from the graves of those from ages 11 to 19 can be used to cause inattentiveness and irresponsible behavior. Try this dirt, too, when you want to stir interest in another person, cause romantic involvement, kindle sexual attraction, and increase sexual prowess.

Adulterer or Adulteress: Use this dirt to cause a love triangle or bring about the urges to cheat on one's spouse. There's nothing more effective for breaking up a romantic involvement.

Child (ages 2–10): This is a terrific aid when the appearance of childlike innocence is a factor, or the development of new friendships is your quest. It's also a great help when obtaining basic necessities is at stake, but for this purpose, it's best to gather the dirt from the grave of a poor child rather than from one who was handed everything on a silver platter.

Doctor: This dirt can be used either to heal or to cause illness, depending upon your intention.

Executed or Murdered: Extremely powerful when it comes to matters of wrongdoing or injustice, this dirt can also be useful in efforts of revenge or those to cause harm to others.

Gambler: If you are sure that the gambler was good at his game, then this dirt can be used to increase luck at the tables, slots, or tracks. If not, use it to force someone to take unnecessary risks—those way beyond the point of reason.

Infant: Since a baby's vision is still somewhat blurry, this dirt is helpful when you need someone to cast a blind eye to something that you're doing. It's also useful if your purpose involves ensuring that someone becomes totally dependent on you, or when you need to appear indispensable.

Insane: This dirt is used for the obvious reason: to cause insanity in another. When collecting it for use, though, remember that you're dealing with the spirit of the mentally infirmed. And just because it agrees to assist you, doesn't mean it will follow through—at least, not in a manner you intend.

Lawyer/Judge: There's little better when it comes to winning a court case or receiving a settlement. It can also be useful if injustice is at issue, or your rights have been violated.

Magical Practitioner: Dirt from this grave can be used for virtually anything.

Nun or Priest: While dirt from these graves is often used for efforts involving personal spiritual protection, it's also used occasionally to convey the appearance of innocent goodness to the outside world.

Pet: Dirt from the grave of your former pet can be used for many things, including protection and loyalty. It's also known to be effective in matters of the heart.

Physically or Emotionally Abused: While this dirt is extremely useful in assisting those in an abusive relationship, its strength lies *only* in giving them the courage to remove themselves from the bad situation. It is not—and I want to be really clear about this—a substitute for picking up the phone and calling the police!

Serial Killer or Murderer: Do not use this dirt unless your intention is to cause serious harm to someone. In fact, its magical incorporation could even cause death.

Soldier: Because soldiers are strong, brave, quick thinkers and are trained to follow orders, dirt from their graves can be used for nearly anything. Before gathering it, though, it's a good idea to note the birthplace and any other data on the headstone that might indicate the causes that he or she believed in and fought for. The last thing you want is dirt from a soldier who might be at cross-purposes, thwart your efforts, or work against you.

Getting the Scoop on Other Dirt

With so much ado about graveyard dirt, most of us automatically assume that nothing else will do—at least not when it comes to working magic. But that's just not so. In fact, there are lots of other places from which you can gather dirt—places, I might add, that are more easily accessible and depending upon your intention, may even suit your purposes better. Best of all, you won't be left in the position of having to explain yourself to local law enforcement if you handle things properly.

But how do you manage that? It's a simple matter of using common sense and keeping your wits about you. Begin by carefully surveying your surroundings and taking special notice of what seems normal for the area. In the case of the courthouse square, for example, you might find people sitting around under trees, eating lunch, and just generally milling around. All you have to do to blend in is act in kind. Plop down under a tree—a book is a handy prop if you've got one available—then idly pick up a stick and proceed to scratch at the ground. You'll have what you need in no time flat, and all without drawing the slightest bit of attention to yourself. You get the idea.

The list below outlines a few alternative locations for dirt collection. And even if you're not concerned about digging around in the cemetery, you may want to give some of them a shot. A brief description of intent follows each for your convenience.

Bank or Financial Institution: Collect and use this dirt to bring money into your hands or to receive payment of a long overdue debt.

Church: This dirt is excellent when used to invite the assistance of positive spiritual forces. It also goes a long way toward protecting against the intrusion of evil spirits.

Courthouse: Use this dirt for anything even remotely involving legal matters. This could include contracts, court cases, general justice, and even money that's owed to you. If your intent would benefit from the discerning eye of the law, this is the dirt you need.

Educational Facility: Whether it comes from a schoolyard or a college campus, this dirt is excellent for efforts involving knowledge acquisition and retention. It can also be used effectively in magic to induce study.

Enemy's Home: Granted, gathering this dirt is a bit trickier and may involve some skulking around to collect. But there's no better way to cut your enemy off at the knees than to use dirt from his own home against him. Just an aside, though: unless you want to cause possible harm to everyone living on that property, be very careful how you word the related spell.

Garden or Flower Shop: Often used in love spells, this dirt has the tendency to make love sprout and grow roots, bud and blossom. Unless you're playing for keeps, though, it's inadvisable to add this dirt to your magic.

Home: Gather this dirt to protect all the occupants of your home and guarantee their safe return. The best way to accomplish this is to sprinkle a bit in every pair of shoes in the house. To ensure that someone else visits you again, sprinkle a bit in his or her shoes.

Hospital, Clinic, or Doctor's Office: Gather dirt from any of these locations for efforts that involve healing. There are a couple of things you should keep in mind, though. First, no magic in the world is a substitute for medical care or prescription medication. And second, be certain that healing is exactly what you've got in mind when you add this dirt to magic, especially if a serious illness is involved and death is a possibility for the recipient. Why? Because healing and staying alive are two entirely different things. And death is often the best way to heal someone.

Jail: Use this dirt to keep the police away from your door, especially if you're prone to trouble with them. To make yourself invisible to the police and perhaps, cause them to overlook a bench warrant, add a piece of hematite to the dirt.

Police Station: Dirt from this area is often collected and sprinkled along the baseboards of the home and along the edges of its structure to keep the family safe from harm. It's not a good idea to use this dirt if you're involved in any sort of illegal activity, though, as it could bring the police straight to your door.

Shopping Center or Mall: These areas are always busy, employ many people, and have a reputation for attracting large amounts of cash. For this reason, there's nothing better than this type of dirt when used in efforts to obtain gainful employment or increase your cash flow.

Workplace: There are lots of uses for this sort of dirt. It works wonders when included in efforts for getting a promotion or raise. But that's not all. It can also be used to foil a coworker or for figuratively getting the dirt on the company, itself.

Charming the Dirt

Now that you've collected the dirt, you'll want to put it to use. And while a good portion of it will probably be added to spells, curses, and ritual supplies like oils, washes, and powders, it's a good idea to use some of the more positive stuff for yourself. After all, one can never have too much good luck. Right? Besides, if you're even thinking along the line of hexes and curses, you'll want to go the extra mile and do whatever it takes to protect yourself.

One of the great things about dirt is that it works of its own accord. You don't have to cleanse it. You don't have to charge it. You don't have to do any of the things you might ordinarily do when using another substance in magical work. The fact that it's a part of the Earth, and thus as old as creation, gives it stability. As it's sucked up the collective consciousness of all who have stepped on it over the years, it has knowledge and power. And if you've collected it from the graveyard, it's also imbued with the energies and qualities of the person whose final resting place you've tapped. Put it all together, and you have a ready-made magical operation. All you have to do is apply it.

There are several ways to do this, but all have the same beginnings. Simply put, you need to decide which dirt samples to combine. You can mix as many or as few as you like, the only rule being that the combination must be to your benefit and not harm you in any way, shape, or form.

Once you've made that decision, the only thing left to figure out is exactly how you intend to apply the dirt. Know that there is no wrong or right way and that you can't screw this up.

Just choose a method with which you're comfortable—even if it's not listed below—and let the dirt do its thing.

Sprinkling: Perhaps the easiest and quickest way to incorporate the dirt's beneficial energies into your life is to sprinkle it along your baseboards, under your rugs, and along the outside perimeter of your property. It's also a good idea to sprinkle it under the doormat and around the front porch. The only drawback with its presence inside the house is the vacuum cleaner. Just know that you'll have to replace the dirt if you decide to embark upon a cleaning frenzy.

Charm Bag: Also known as a mojo and sometimes a gris gris, this bag is traditionally made of red flannel, but it's frequently constructed of other materials such as leather, beadwork, and more decorative fabrics by today's practitioners. The dirt is usually combined with snippets of your hair and fingernail clippings (these taglocks identify you as the person to reap the rewards), along with any other items you consider of benefit. The entire mixture is then placed into the bag, which is worn around the neck or someplace else close to the body. These bags also may contain taglocks from other family members. In that case, though, the bag should be buried rather than worn and rest as close to the front step of the home as possible.

Good-Luck Bottle: Sometimes known as a Witch's Bottle, this generally takes the form of a jar with a tight-fitting screw-on lid. The dirt mixture is placed in the bottom of the container and sprinkled with herbs that vibrate to good fortune. (Any combination may be used, but I tend to use cinnamon, basil, and lavender, as they bring love, money, and spiritual protection.) Traditionally, fishhooks are also added to "hook" good luck, as are nine dimes in payment to the spirit world for its protection and rewards. Once the jar is at least half full, it should be filled to the top with your urine, capped tightly, and buried on your property—preferably as close to the front door as possible.

Garden Additive: While I've also heard of practitioners adding the dirt mixture to the soil in their flowerbeds and vegetable gardens, I've never tried this myself. However, the premise is that as the plants grow, so do the rewards to the beneficiary. And in the case of vegetables, "ingesting" the good luck would seem a most appropriate way of having said luck become an integral part of not only one's life, but also, in essence, of oneself.

Chapter 3

The Curse of the 11" Fashion Doll

1959 was an auspicious year. Mattel moved a new girl to town and brought her out to play. Gorgeous, fun-loving and intelligent, the 11" fashion doll befriended all who sought her out. And if that weren't thrilling enough, her not-too-shabby boyfriend seemed perfectly willing to come along for the ride. Little girls everywhere were absolutely beside themselves and couldn't wait to take her home. (Parents were happy too, for at $1.98, most of them could afford to buy her.)

Of course, only the toy company realized that the dolls were really magic come to fruition. Parents hadn't yet figured out that buying the doll was just the beginning. Or that normal modes of punishment weren't even going to begin to stop their daughters' whines once they had the doll in hand. No, the only solution was to go for broke, mortgage the house, and acquire that million-dollar wardrobe so befitting a pony-tailed length of plastic with a teeny-tiny price tag and a waist to match.

The folks at Mattel sure knew their stuff, all right. Who else, after all, could cast a spell so powerful that its effects would outlast its original magicians? But even though they'd conjured some powerful magic in invention, marketing, sales, and sidelines—to say nothing of invoking the necessary mid-wifing skills to birth such a large neighborhood of fashionable friends—it's a safe bet that they failed to see the whole picture. Or at least the part of it that offered more than a set of dolls with expensive clothing. If they hadn't, there wouldn't be a cheap knockoff anywhere. And yet, hundreds of them line the shelves of corner dollar stores all over the world.

That's good news for magical practitioners. Why? Because it gives us a quick, easy, and inexpensive alternative to bean-bags, carved potatoes, and grapevine figures with Spanish moss tresses. It allows us to put aside our sewing kits and save those stacks of felt scraps for other purposes. But even bet-ter—at least for clumsy practitioners like me—it puts an end to the inadvertent blood sacrifice that too often accompanies the slipped rotary blade or knife.

That's right, folks! That lovely little fashion doll—the very same one who joyfully befriended all who sought her out—has now become the magical practitioner's best friend as well. Used properly, she's become the perfect poppet. The quintessential poppet. The ready-made poppet that's just waiting to go home with you and be molded to your specifications. And all for less than a good cup of coffee. What could be better than that?

True enough, you may not be able to find a doll that meets all your specifications when it comes to acquiring a poppet. But that's not a problem. Creativity is not only the matrix from which all magic flows, it's also the stuff that nurtures the child in each of us and encourages it to have fun. And when it comes right down to it, it's that child we're avenging anytime a hex or curse comes into play. So, bring forth that child, unleash its creative urges, and let's have some fun!

The Magical Poppeteer

When using the fashion doll as a poppet, it's important that the doll somewhat resemble the person in question. Somewhat is key here, though, so don't get caught up in the but-it-doesn't-look-exactly-like cycle. Such will only serve to make you crazy, and that will defeat your purpose. Just remember that if *you* know who the doll is supposed to represent, so will the Powers Who Be. And in this case, that's all that matters.

That said, let's start with hair and eye color. The best possible scenario is, of course, to find a doll whose hair and eye colors both match those of the object of your intentions. But as that's not always possible, check for hair color first.

There are a couple of reasons for this. For one thing, hair color is just as much a part of a person's individuality as the curve of the toenail. For another, snippets of hair have, for centuries, been used to identify objects of intent during spell-casting. And since the poppet is a symbol of that object, it's imperative to get as close to the proper shade as possible.

As simple as it sounds, this can occasionally present a few problems. You may know, for example, that the person in question is the queen or king of hair dye, that the only one privy to the natural shade is a well-tipped hairdresser, and that nothing—not even pain of death—is going to pry it out of them. Not to worry. Just purchase a doll tressed in the current shade and call it good.

On the other hand, what you may really need is a doll with silver hair, and for obvious reasons, the chances of finding one are slim to none. That's not as much of a problem as it might seem either. Just take a good look at the person's coloring. That will give you a clue as to the shade with which the person was born, and you can go from there.

Of course, it may be that you've already searched through multiple dollar stores for a redheaded wonder, there's none to be found, and you simply don't have time to drive all over hell and half of Georgia to locate one. What then? Just relax and take a deep breath. Then grab the doll with the palest hair in the store, march over to the section touting permanent markers—these little goodies are great for coloring hair—select the proper shade, and head for the checkout counter.

With that out of the way, let's move on to eye color. And since manufacturers tend to pair certain hair and eye colors together, the search for a doll with the right combination of shades may be a moot point. There's no need to despair, though. Paint pens are the answer. Just a dab or two and you're good to go. End of problem.

There is one other thing that some practitioners tend to worry about when it comes to finding the proper poppet. And as much as I hate to even mention it, that worrisome characteristic is skin color. So, let's address that now and get it out of the way. If you can find a doll with the proper skin tone, grab it and consider yourself lucky. But if you can't, don't spend a lot of time searching. Don't make a problem where there isn't one. And for the love of the Gods, don't overanalyze. Just know that by the time you're done with preparations, there won't be any question as to who your poppet represents. I personally guarantee it.

Tools of the Trade

Now that you've got the poppet, it's time to gather some supplies. What you'll actually need, however, depends on two very important factors:

1. What the object of your intent actually looks like; and

2. How you intend to use the poppet.

If the object of your intent wears glasses, for example, you might need fine-tipped markers to draw them on the doll's face. If a severe adjustment in body shape is necessary, art or modeling clay would be useful. Adding duct or electrical tape—or maybe even ribbons—to your supply list could be in order if you're planning a binding. But if you're not, there's no need to bother with them. You get the idea.

That said, a list of possible preparation tools and supplies follows below, as well as ideas for using them. Don't stop here though. Be creative and use whatever feels right to you. Remember: This is your poppet, and your curse. And your magical signature should be all over it.

> **Permanent markers:** Regardless of how you're using the poppet, these are a multipurpose preparation staple. Because you'll use these for everything from labeling the poppet with the object's name to adding identifying marks (tattoos, birthmarks, and even glasses come to mind here), it's a good idea to keep an assortment of colors in a variety of tip widths.

> **Scissors:** If your object of intent has short hair and the poppet has long, flowing tresses, a haircut may be in order.

You'll also need these for cutting lengths of ribbon, cord, or other binding materials.

Art or modeling clay: This can come in handy if the object of your intent doesn't possess the lean, curvy body of your poppet. Just add a bit here and there to manufacture beer bellies, sagging butts, and those winged upper arms.

Duct or electrical tape: There's simply nothing better when it comes to binding a poppet. But that's just the beginning. Use it as a blind to force the object of your intent into complete oblivion or as a gag to stop diarrhea of the mouth. Don't discount slapping a piece across the nose either—especially if nosiness is an issue.

Ribbon or cord: Some practitioners prefer this for binding, as it allows for the use of knot work.

Related herbs, oils, etc.: To add some extra punch to your intention, you may want to rub the poppet with these or add them to the head or body cavities.

Cotton balls or fiberfill: Use as body cavity stuffing to keep herbs and oils in place.

Pen and paper: If you want the object of your intent to be mindful of a particular thought, just write it on a piece of paper, and slip it inside the head cavity.

Since this list isn't by any means complete, you may want to add other supplies as well. Some practitioners, for instance, like to sew clothes for their poppets—and if that's the case with you, a trip to the fabric store might be in order. Other practitioners like to add accessories related to their intent, so this might call for any number of items from the arts and crafts store. Still other practitioners wouldn't dream of turning a poppet loose on the world without first sealing its harm away from unsuspecting innocents, and such a ritual might mean the addition of candles, Element symbols, or other ritual tools. So use your intuition when it comes to gathering your supplies, and know that whatever it tells you will be absolutely right for your specific intent and purpose.

A Poppet by Any Other Name

Sometimes, a poppet doesn't really need any preparation for magical use at all. (If you were simply working toward a round of wild, hot, passionate jungle sex, for example, preparations might only entail tying two dolls of the appropriate genders together with red ribbon, putting them under your bed, and calling it good.) But such is not the case when using the poppet in a curse. That's because the Universe needs to know exactly who the poppet represents and who to target. But there's more to it than that. It also needs to know what course of action to take. And as this is serious business, there truly is no room for doubt in either area.

Of course, this means that no matter what your intention is, you'll need those permanent markers I mentioned in the supply list. Why? Because to avoid confusing the Universe, you'll want to clearly label the doll with the name of your intended. And the last thing you need—especially when a curse is involved—is for the identifying factor to rub or wear off.

It's also a good idea to label the doll with your intended's legal name. And since we live in an era where people hide behind internet nicknames, that may take a little research. No need to despair, though. Just ask around. The information may be easier to get than you think.

Once you've got a name, use a permanent marker to write it clearly and neatly down the length of one of the doll's legs. Then write the nickname—if any—down the other leg. This way there won't be any mistake as to your object of intent.

But what if you've exhausted all possibilities, and you still can't uncover a legal name? Does that mean that the poppet won't work?

No. There are other options. And while I wouldn't recommend them unless all else fails, the following do provide workable solutions.

- Obtain a photograph of the person in question. Secure a length of ribbon or twine to the upper corners and hang it around the doll's neck.

- Use an email or a letter from the offending party as an identifier. Just print it out, trim away your name, and fold the paper as many times as possible. Then use duct or electrical tape to secure it to the doll's body.

- If neither of those provide a viable option, just label the doll with the name by which you know the person and call it good. Know, though, that you'll have to strengthen your focus, clearly visualizing the person—or summoning up the "feel" of his or her personal energy—while working on the doll.

Personal Marks to Fuel the Sparks

Now that there's no mistaking the poppet's identity, grab those supplies and let the creative juices flow. It's time to have a little fun. Yes . . . it's time to accessorize. And when working with poppets, this can mean virtually anything from adding personal marks to the doll's body to making a fashion statement.

But let's start with the personal marks. If you know that the person in question has a birthmark or permanent body art, add those to the doll, using your markers. Not to worry if you don't have any artistic talent. That's not what this is about. Instead, it's about fixing the image of the person in your mind's eye, and you don't have to be an artist to do that. Simply draw something—anything, even if it's only a stick picture—on the areas of the body you know are tattooed. Do the same with any other identifying marks. (Moles, scars, and freckles come to mind here.)

Don't stop there, though. It's also a good time to add any symbols that represent your curse. Want to instill confusion? Draw a series of question marks on the forehead. Want the subject to feel absolutely awful about screwing you over? Just draw a broken heart on the chest area. How about curtailing that sexual harassment at the workplace? A large red X drawn across the genital area definitely goes a long way toward drying up those urges.

That's all well and fine. But what if it's not that easy? What if you're dealing with the sneaky sort, the sort who's a pro at hiding true colors and always comes out smelling like a rose? What sort of symbol could ever snare a snake like that?

It's not as difficult as it may seem. All you need is a little illumination. And while drawing a symbol on the doll probably won't do the trick, that fine, glittery faery dust will. Just brush it all over the doll, paying special attention to the face. After you're done, even a blind man could pick your subject out of a crowd! Guaranteed.

The Personality Factor

Once you're satisfied with the doll's markings, you need to make a few decisions. First on the agenda, though, is whether to stop right where you are, or continue to accessorize. If you're not sure, then ask yourself the following question: Does the poppet truly reflect your subject's personality?

If the answer is no, then give some thought to what's missing. Maybe it's a fragrance, a signature hair accoutrement, or a certain piece of jewelry. (If you're looking for body jewelry, jump rings from the arts and crafts store make wonderful substitutes.) It could be a specific kind of shoe (these can easily be drawn onto the feet and colored in), an object they carry around constantly (legal pads, books, a handbag), or a pen that seems to have found a permanent home over the right ear. There's also the possibility that the missing factor is something even more subtle. It could be an attitude, or that deep, dark wrinkle in the middle of the forehead.

Still can't figure it out? Just keep playing with it—adding and subtracting items—until the doll seems right. Given enough thought, it will all come together. And you'll definitely know when it does.

Fashion Plate or Naked Wonder?

Remember that fashion statement we touched on earlier? Well, now's the time to decide whether or not you want to dress the poppet. There's no real rule of thumb here, and I've seen good arguments for both. Some folks say that stripping the poppet and leaving it bare aids and abets the Universe in its work. Besides, this is a curse we're talking about, and the last thing on your mind should be giving the object of your intent any comfort. Wouldn't it be more fitting to leave the subject cold and miserable, and symbolically exposed to the Elements? Perhaps.

Others, however, stringently disagree. They say that dressing the poppet in the same sort of attire as the person it represents narrows the Universal search. Giving the Universe some direction and a starting point saves time. And anything that saves time makes life easier. Then they quickly point out that making life easier is the reason that people work magic in the first place. End of argument.

So, who's right and who's wrong?

All and none.

The fact of the matter is that both sectors have good points, and both methods work equally well. It's just a matter of deciding which way you want to go with this. So, trust your instincts, and know that you've made the right choice. Don't be surprised, though, if your decision varies from poppet to poppet. That's to be expected, as each situation is different.

If you do decide to dress the poppet, you may want to schedule the clothing search early—perhaps even before locating the doll. (Online doll sites and auction sites are good bets.) The reason is simple. Once folks start working on their poppet, they tend to gather a sort of magical momentum. Since that momentum plays an integral role in fueling the curse, you won't want to lose it. And that's exactly what could happen if you stop the process to look for clothing. (The time gap could be even longer if you decide to get out the sewing machine.)

Depending upon what you've got in mind, though, you may not even need to search for doll clothes. One of my friends insists that dressing a poppet in rags symbolizes the subject's downfall. And if that's a path you'd like to travel, all you'll need is an old cleaning rag. Just tear it into strips, then wrap and tie them in a few strategic places. The doll is all dressed and ready to go.

Making the Doll Walk and Talk

Oh, come now. You didn't really believe that, did you? All the magic in the world isn't going to make your doll walk or talk—not literally anyway. But I damned sure got your attention. And that's exactly what I wanted to do; for this is the most exciting part of working with the fashion doll, and you can't afford to miss a single word of it!

Yes, this is where the fashion doll really outshines its cousin, the handmade poppet. It's not that it's more lifelike or more durable and has nothing to do with its beauty or time-saving qualities. No, it's something else entirely. Something that is, to the magical practitioner, an absolute joy but tends to go completely unnoticed.

I have to admit that I didn't notice it either, until my dear friend, author M. R. Sellars, pointed it out to me several years ago.

It was one of those days where nothing went right, and I'd just wished the Gods had had enough sense to cancel the entire twenty-four-hour period. And to top it off, I realized that I was being screwed out of some money. Not just a little money, mind you. I'm talking about a *lot* of money—and for a Taurus, that's no minor infraction. Truth be told, to most of those who share my astrological sign, not even punishment by death, itself, is stringent enough to fit that crime.

So, there I was: pacing back and forth like a caged coyote, dreaming up ways to get my money. Lots of ideas came to mind, of course—they always do—but nothing I could think of was going to work the way I wanted. You see, it wasn't just the money at stake. The fact that I'd been screwed over was an issue too. And that meant that performing a good old-fashioned money spell simply wouldn't do. In this case, my satisfaction hinged on two conditions: First, the money had to come from its initial source; and second, there had to be retribution. Stout retribution. Swift retribution. Enough retribution that those folks would never dare to mess with me again. By the time I was done, I wanted them to rue the day they'd ever heard my name.

I turned on my heel to march back across the room for the umpteenth time and caught Sellars watching me from his seat at the dining room table. I cocked an eyebrow in his direction and stopped dead in my tracks.

"What?!"

"Nothin'," he replied. "Just wonderin' how long you're gonna keep that up."

"Until I come up with a solution," I said as my feet fell into rhythm again. "A good solution. A satisfactory solution. A solution that will . . . "

"How about a poppet?"

"Thought of that. But it's not going to make 'em write that check."

He ran his finger down the side of his goatee and nodded his head thoughtfully, a sure sign that all his brain cells were firing to capacity. "Oh, yeah, it could," he said, a slow grin spreading across his face. "You've just gotta work it right."

Well, that was enough to bring me to a screeching halt. But even if it hadn't been, what came next would surely have done the trick. He had a solution, all right. And to think: it had been staring me right in the face the whole time.

Got Cavities?

The first order of business was just the normal stuff: I had to design a poppet that looked like the woman who wrote the checks. And while the next thing on the list took a bit more work, it was neither a problem nor out of the ordinary. It only involved constructing a miniature checkbook complete with a check that was made payable to me, securing it in her left hand, and securing a miniature pen in her other.

But the rest of it involved utilizing an absolute treasure trove of endless magical possibility. Something that, sadly enough, most of us don't ever notice. And if Sellars hadn't pointed them out to me, I'd still be oblivious to the existence of these precious little gems or their many uses. But once he did, it was like turning me loose in a jewelry store with a bottomless wallet. I could believe neither my good fortune nor the fact that I had managed to miss something so blatantly obvious. And neither will you. For the priceless commodities in question are none other than those lovely, empty body cavities—just waiting to be filled with whatever magic the heart desires. And when it comes to curses, nothing could be better.

Fact is, these empty spaces truly can be stuffed with anything imaginable. Want someone to think certain thoughts? Then write them on slips of paper and toss them into the head cavity. Want the object of your intentions to have an upset belly every time he treats you poorly? Just stuff the body cavity with cotton, pour in a little vinegar, and know that nausea, indigestion, and gastric disorders are on the way.

See how simple that is? And it's only the beginning. For your convenience, other ideas follow below. Use them as a guideline, add a bit of imagination, and see just how far they take you. You'll be positively amazed. Guaranteed!

Head Cavity

Plain cotton: To cause sinus trouble, lightheadedness, faulty decision-making.

Sugared or honey-soaked cotton: To inspire your enemy to think sweet thoughts of you.

Thorns or grass burrs: To induce headache.

Mugwort: To cause one to be oblivious to your actions.

Jimson weed, belladonna, or monkshood: To cause madness, induce paranoia, and bring on erratic and delusional behavior.

Valerian: To bring on apathy and inertia.

Feathers: To induce long bouts of sneezing and coughing.

Rocks: To relieve clarity of mind and induce stupidity.

Mustard, red jasper and slippery elm: To stop gossip and speaking out of turn.

Chest Cavity

(Note: depending upon the doll, it may be necessary to stuff the stomach cavity with cotton in order to secure items in this area.)

Plain cotton: To cause chest congestion.

Water-soaked cotton: To bring on pneumonia, bronchitis, and other respiratory problems.

Ammonia-soaked cotton: To induce shortness of breath.

Foxglove: To cause heart palpitations.

Black onyx: To cause breakup in a relationship. Add a paper heart ripped in half if heartbreak is desired.

Stomach Cavity

Tangled threads: To figuratively tie the belly in knots.

Mint: Place low in the belly to cause impotence. (Great for cases of sexual harassment.)

Coins: To cause the target to become sickened by his or her greed.

Symbols representative of the target's misdeeds: To cause an upset stomach each and every time the target tries to behave inappropriately.

The Nurse's Curse

While the poppet is normally used to put others in their places and curb their abilities to do you harm, that's not the only area in which it excels. And even though this little tidbit does, indeed, fall under the heading of curses, it's one designed to work for the good of all. In fact, some folks might even prefer to put it in the category of healing.

The truth of the matter is that the one thing that scares us most is the possibility of personal illness—or even worse, becoming totally incapacitated because of it. And that's because it's the one thing over which we have little control. We're seldom sure exactly how we managed to get that way or how to squelch it. Our only hope is that the doctor has more of a clue than we do. Which, unfortunately, is not always the case. As a result, we're left feeling completely vulnerable, thoroughly exposed, and absolutely terrified. And that's no way to live.

The poppet, however, can be of some assistance when used to curse the very disease that's causing you so much trouble. And while it's not by any stretch of the imagination a replacement for good medical care—nothing is—it can go a long way toward squelching the problem and assisting with the healing process when used in conjunction with the prescribed treatment. What could be better than that?

The process is a relatively simple one and begins with designing the poppet. The only exception here is that you'll fashion the poppet after yourself. Once that's done, check online or head to the library for a picture of the part of your body that's diseased. If the internal organs are involved—and they usually are—you'll need depictions of the specific organs affected. (It's imperative that the likenesses you choose are of normal, healthy organs and/or fully functioning body parts.) Then make two copies of each picture, and put one set aside for later use.

Now pinpoint the area of affliction on each picture, and completely color that area with a black marker to represent the disease. Then cover the area with a large red X, and deliver your curse. You might ball the paper up in your fist, stomp on it, rip it to shreds, burn it to ashes, or all of the above. Just do whatever appeals to you. And when you're finished? Toss the remnants in the toilet, urinate on them, and flush to symbolize the disease leaving your body.

When you're done, shrink the other set of pictures to doll size, cut them out, and place them in the appropriate areas of the poppet's body. Put the poppet where you see it often, and spend a bit of time each day visualizing your body returning to normalcy, increasing in strength, and glowing with good health.

A Breath of Fresh Air

By now the doll's been marked and adorned, stuffed and dressed. It's all ready to go. Right? Well . . . some practitioners say yes. Others say there's one more step you need to take before turning the poppet loose to do its stuff. And whether you want to go there or not is entirely up to you.

So, what is this final step?

It's breathing life into the doll, so it can more easily make the connection to its human counterpart and start doing its thing.

I have to admit that I was a little hesitant about including this material because I'm of the opinion that it can be downright dangerous. Please don't misunderstand, though. It's not putting the information out there that concerns me, as I truly believe that refusal to do so only contributes to faulty decision-making. Instead, it's knowing what folks normally tend to do with this information—or not do, as the case may be—once I've shared it.

You see, in order to follow this step properly, you must initiate a death date.

Granted, said death date is only for the life of the poppet. But people seem to have a real problem with this. Maybe the D-word scares the hell out of them. Maybe they just get attached to their poppets. Or maybe they even worry senselessly that in killing off the poppet, they might also manage to kill their target. Whatever the reason, though, most of them simply refuse to follow through. And that refusal can cause the biggest mess you've ever seen. What's more, it's not a mess that's easily straightened out or whisked away.

Breathing life into a poppet truly does give it a life of its own. No, it won't walk and talk—we've discussed that before—but the energy with which it's imbued will take on form, become an elemental of sorts, and use the doll as its dwelling space. The good news is that it's a stout lackey, capable of doing its job both efficiently and expediently. The bad news is that unless a time limit is set for the task at hand—this is where the death date comes in—it also has a tendency to drag things out and dillydally in the hopes of extending its life cycle. (You're not, after all, likely to destroy it before it completes the job you've set out for it.)

This might not be so bad except for a couple of things. First and foremost, you want your instructions carried out immediately. If you didn't, you wouldn't have designed the poppet to start with. But the second thing is what makes this action so dangerous: The longer the elemental lives, the stronger it gets.

It becomes capable of things you never imagined—things like taking on a mind of its own and devising and carrying out its own plans, whether you like them or not. It becomes totally capable of wreaking havoc in your life and putting you in situations that aren't easily rectified. Yes, left to its own devices, the elemental runs amuck. And once it's strong enough to do that, there's very little that you or anyone else can do to stop it. It's like Frankenstein on steroids. And causing its demise is really going to take some doing.

That said, I urge you to either follow the instructions by setting a death date—and firmly stating such—at the onset of creating this thoughtform, or leave well enough alone. And if you choose the latter? Just perform the Poppet Activation Ritual included in this chapter, and know that the poppet will still do its job per your instructions. It may just take a bit longer. However, there are some things that are well worth the wait.

Creating the Poppet's Assistant

Materials:

> *1 candle in a color appropriate to your intent*
> *Queen of the Whole F***ing Universe*
> > *Incense (see recipe in Chapter 5)*
> *Table salt*
> *Water*
> *Poppet*

Set up the altar as is normal for you, place the poppet in front of the candle, and light the candle and incense.

Blow your breath upon the poppet's body to fill it with the Air Element, paying special attention to the face area. Continue to infuse it with Air until you feel that it's fully charged. (Two or three minutes should do it.) Pass it through the incense smoke and say:

I give you Air to breathe,

Pass the poppet through the candle flame and say:

I grant you the Flame of passion,

Sprinkle the poppet with water and say:

I infuse you with the Waters of Life,

Sprinkle the poppet with salt and say:

I grant you the fertility of Earth.

Then, holding the poppet in your hands, say:

You are now my assistant: I give you direction,
Your life shall be ended at my sole discretion.
My instructions you'll follow, my rules you shall heed,
You'll obey to the letter with vigor and speed.
Assistant you are and assistant you'll be,
Take the life that I give you and be useful to me.
As I will and direct, so shall it be.

Now, still holding the poppet, set a death date and time of death, and state it aloud. Explain to the assistant that this is the length of time allotted to accomplish its task. Then, to ensure the safety of your target, also state that the assistant's demise shall not influence that of your intended subject.

Place the poppet back in front of the candle, visualize precisely what it is that you want the assistant to do, and give it instructions in the form of the curse you've prepared. (If the curse takes the form of a spell—and it probably does—perform it now.) Leave the poppet in front of the candle until the wick extinguishes itself, and know that the assistant will set about tending to the business at hand.

Poppet Activation Ritual

Materials:

>*1 white candle*
>*Activation Incense (see recipe in Chapter 5)*
>*Table salt*
>*Water*
>*Poppet*

Set up the altar as is normal for you, then light the candle and incense. Pass the poppet through the incense smoke, saying:

>*I bless you with Air,*
>*Winds blown cold and winds blown fair.*

Pass the poppet through the candle flame, saying:

>*I bless you with the kiss of Fire*
>*That burns in all with hot desire.*

Sprinkle the poppet with water, saying:

>*I bless you with the Waters of Life,*
>*Both gentle trickles and raging strife.*

Sprinkle the poppet with salt, saying:

>*With Earth, I bless you now at last,*
>*Forest, field, and mountain pass.*

Then place the poppet in front of the candle, hold your hands over it, and charge it by saying something like:

Poppet, with this consecration,
You become (name of your target)'*s representation.*
Every thought I send your way
Will in his/her life begin to play.
Every action befalling you
Will befall (name of your target) *just as true.*
As if s/he were actually in your place,
By my will, though, not a trace
Of harm shall come to anyone
Except for (name of target). *By Moon and Sun,*
By Wind and Flame, by Land and Sea,
As I will, so shall it be!

Leave the poppet in front of the candle until the wick extinguishes itself, then proceed with your prepared curse.

Now What?

You've activated the doll, applied the curse, and the poppet is busily doing its thing and carrying out your wishes. Life is good and you couldn't be happier. There's only one little glitch: The poppet is still living on your altar.

Fact of the matter is that you just can't leave it there indefinitely. You're going to have to do something with it. Put it away somewhere. Find it new living quarters. Get it out of the way. Otherwise, there's eventually going to be a space problem.

But even if that weren't the case, you wouldn't want the poppet just hanging around, infusing your space with its energy. To allow that is tantamount to inviting your target to live with you. And since you certainly don't want that—if you did, you'd never have initiated a curse—it's imperative that the energy be sealed away from you. This means that you're going to have to dispose of the poppet.

There are several ways you can do this, and for your convenience, I've outlined the most common methods below. Since all work equally well, just choose the one with which you're most comfortable, and know that your worries are over.

Disposal by Earth

As you may have guessed, this method involves burying the poppet and is a very simple process. It's only a matter of digging a hole, tossing in the doll, adding a little graveyard dirt and covering it up. Because the doll isn't biodegradable, though, most folks don't want to go there.

There is, however, a more environmentally conscious solution. Just place the doll in a small box (a cigarette carton works well), sprinkle it well with graveyard dirt, and seal the container by covering it completely with duct tape. You can then either put it in your freezer or take it to the dumpster with your trash.

Disposal by Water

While the original method was as easy as tossing the poppet into a body of running water—or maybe, even the sewer—there's a more environmentally conscious way of doing this too. Just place the doll in an empty quart milk carton, cover with Swamp Water (see recipe in Chapter 5), and seal well with duct tape. Then toss it in your freezer and forget about it.

Don't want the poppet living in your freezer? Well, there's an alternative to this too, provided you have the time and space to utilize it. Since Swamp Water literally eats away at the poppet, you can also place the doll in a bucket filled with the substance (be sure to fill the body cavities with the liquid to prevent floating), cover the top, and leave it outside until the whole mess dissolves. Know, though, that you may have to add more Swamp Water before the process is completed.

Disposal by Fire

This is, by far, the easiest and least time-consuming method of all. Just build a fire in your cauldron—either with wood or charcoal briquettes—and toss the doll on the pyre. Tend the fire until the poppet is past the melting point and is nothing but ash, then bury the ashes when cool.

As a preventative measure, though, you'll want to clean your cauldron thoroughly after using it in this fashion. Scrub it well with steel wool and rubbing alcohol, then wash as usual with soap and hot water. You also may want to oil it before putting it away.

Disposal by Air

This method of disposal is definitely easy, but as it requires a trip to an isolated area, it may take some advance planning. Once you get to the place of your choice, all you have to do is leave the doll there, exposed to the Elements, and walk away. It's important, however, that you don't look back.

Chapter 4

Immersing the Curse

My sister and I are both avid readers. We enjoy the same subject matter. We like the same writing styles. And as such, we frequently suggest books and authors to each other. We also tend to wind up in bookstores during our annual visits, and because we're rather noisy—our exuberant exclamations of "Have you read this?" "This book's to die for!" and "This author will absolutely scare the bejesus out of you!" resound through the store—it's a wonder that we haven't been eighty-sixed from all of them. But putting up with our antics is probably a small price to pay, since by the time we're done, we each usually walk out with at least two or more shopping bags crammed with books, and the store's been paid handsomely for hosting a few hours of "Sisters Run Amuck."

At any rate, one year's annual visit took place in North Carolina, and we wound up our last day together by visiting a local bookstore. My sister was looking for a specific title—it was something that she desperately wanted me to read—but couldn't find it. I told her it was no big deal. She begged to differ. I shrugged it off at first, but she was so adamant that I finally checked the computer, only to find that it was out of print.

Of course, this started a whole new thread of conversation. She quizzed me on sources for out-of-print books. I admitted that I had a few, and she insisted that I get in touch with them immediately. She said I had to find this book. And when I asked her why? She simply grinned at me and said I needed it. So, I jotted down the information and tossed it in my purse.

To say that I put off finding the novel would be putting it mildly. I had a ton of things to do—tour dates to book, writing to finish, and query letters to send out, just to name a few—and I already had novels enough to entertain me for a few months. So, the truth of the matter is that I forgot all about it. At least, until a package arrived from my sister.

And there it was: *Stitches in Time* by Barbara Michaels.

Now common courtesy would dictate that I read it immediately, especially after she'd gone to all that trouble. But even if that weren't the case, something else should have spurred me into action. You see, my sister is a very magical person. She tends to know things that she doesn't even realize she knows. So when she says something to me, I know to pay heed. But for whatever reason, I didn't. Instead, I just put the book at the bottom of the stack on my bedside table and left it there until I got around to it.

Several weeks later, I sat down to begin actively writing *Utterly Wicked* and hit a stumbling block. I couldn't decide whether I really wanted to write the chapter you're currently reading. It had seemed like a good idea at the onset. What, after all, could be more intriguing than weaving a curse into some seemingly harmless object? Something so ordinary and so innocuous that safe use would never come into question? I also felt sure that just this sort of thing had been done by practitioners for as long as they'd existed on the face of the Earth. Still, I wasn't sure I had enough material to write a whole chapter. And I knew that my chances of finding someone with firsthand knowledge who'd actually be willing to discuss this with me were definitely slim to none.

After much debate and no resolution, I finally decided to take a break. My hope, of course, was that the solution would come when I wasn't actively dwelling on it, and the best way I knew to take my mind off the problem was to engross myself in a good book. So, I grabbed the first novel on the stack and, much to my surprise, discovered it was none other than *Stitches in Time*.

I wasn't even through the first chapter when I understood why my sister had been so insistent and had gone to so much trouble. For there, between the covers, a story of magical needlework lived and breathed. But it wasn't just an ordinary story. It was the story of an antique wedding quilt, pieced and stitched by a spurned lover and given to the bride of the man who had jilted her. And wouldn't you just know it?! Finely stitched into each and every block lay individual curses. Curses amplified by several layers of graveyard dirt worked into the batting. Curses that had taken on a life of their own, gathered momentum, and managed to survive for more than a hundred years.

Well, after reading that book, one thing was clear: I definitely needed to write this chapter, as no book on curses would be complete without it. Of course, I still didn't have contact information for the experts I'd need for my research, but I decided not to worry about that. I learned a long time ago that experts tend to find me when I'm ready for them. And, believe it or not . . . they did!

The Magic Built Within a Quilt

Most everyone loves quilts. There's nothing quite like curling up beneath one to make you feel cozy and loved. They make you feel better when you're sick as a dog. And with today's hand-dyed fabrics in a plethora of brilliant colors, they are often real works of art, delighting all who view them with their lovely patterns of patchwork and stitches.

So, how could any one object manage all of this and be anything less than magical?

The answer is simple: It can't.

Some practitioners define magic as the change of any condition by ritual means, and the quilt definitely meets those terms. For one thing, the piece is constructed of fabric that is woven from thread. Thread is spun from fiber that, even in this day and time, is often obtained from plants and animals and thus carries the energies of its source. And because of all the changes in condition—rituals, if you will—necessary to create fabric, some of these practitioners believe that all cloth, in and of itself, is magical.

Of course, some of them don't embrace that theory. They do, however, agree that once fabrics are removed from their bolts, cut apart, and pieced back together to create something new and different, the rituals involved definitely constitute a magical operation.

Other practitioners disagree stringently, but that's because they take the definition of magic one step further. They insist that, for magic to occur, the change of condition must be effected by unseen forces. And it's those folks who look at the rest of us as if we've lost our minds, pat us on the heads like small children, and inform us that quilts—because every change in condition involved can be seen with the naked eye—are simply not in the running.

Okay . . . I'll defend their right to believe anything they wish. But it's all I can do to stop myself from screaming "Bullshit!" right in their little self-righteous faces.

The fact of the matter is that they're missing the point. Everything that someone touches carries their invisible mark, their energy, and their vibration. And nothing, during its creation, is handled or touched more than a quilt. Every stitch carries the thought processes, attitudes, and emotional content of its maker. Those things definitely change the condition. And it's those things that make it magical.

But let's go a little further with this and talk about sleep. There we are, lying in bed, in a state of suspended animation. We have no control over anything. Not our snoring, our drooling, or our dreams. And because of that, it's the one time during every twenty-four-hour period when we are absolutely, positively, without a doubt vulnerable.

Now, put us under a quilt during that time of vulnerability, and what happens? Just as the quilt embraces us to form a cocoon of cozy warmth, all of the quilt maker's invisible imprints—every emotion, every thought, and every attitude—do as well. They seep right into our very pores. They become a part of us and we a part of them. And that, my friends, is true magic in progress.

A Curse by Design: The Patch of Nine

The knowledge that every quilt (and every stitchery project, as well) is inherently magical is just the beginning: It's the base with which we start and the foundation upon which we build. It's what we decide to do with that project and how we decide to work with it that determines the magic that will live within. And that starts with design.

One of my favorite designs (shown below) is a very old and simple one known as the nine-patch, which provides powerful magic regardless of intent.

As each block employs three rows of three squares, the design automatically includes a visual spell binding of sorts—a binding that many practitioners know as the binding of three times three and used to seal their magical operations as well as to prevent them from backfiring. The most commonly used version was penned by Starhawk in *The Spiral Dance* and goes like this:

"By all the power of three times three
This spell bound around shall be
To cause no harm or return on me
As I will, so mote it be!"

And having a representative spell binding already worked into the project is definitely a plus when it comes to hexes and curses.

Another reason the nine-patch is a good choice is that, just as the name implies, nine pieces are used to construct the block. Nine, of course, is the number frequently associated with wishes, and in some cultures, it's even associated with general success. And since successful manifestation of your intent and wishes is precisely what's desired during magical work, there's no better symbol to incorporate.

But that's not all. One of the main reasons I like to use this particular design in curses is because the whole block pattern consists of squares. Aside from the fact that the square has many possibilities when it comes to symbolism—balance between the right- and left-hand paths, the Elements, the primary directions, and so forth—it can also be used to box your target in with whatever you've manifested. It's like locking the door and throwing away the key, and renders any attempt to avoid the associated magic completely futile.

While all of those are very good reasons to use the nine-patch in your work, there is one thing more about this versatile little block that truly seals the deal. Because the square has long been utilized to symbolize the Earth, it not only gives your magic the stability of solid ground in which to grow, but grounds your work as well. And this makes it the perfect base from which to form a curse.

That's all well and fine. But what if quilting isn't your thing? What if you're simply not handy with a needle? Does that mean that you can't use this wonderful symbolism in your magic?

Absolutely not. While patchwork and quilting are the most commonly used mediums for employing the nine-patch, there are numerous other ways to incorporate it. And since no artistic talent is necessary to draw the design—all it takes

is a pencil and a ruler and some paints to make it attractive—
you can apply it to nearly anything suitable to gifting. Just be
creative and summon your imagination. The ideas below will
get you started.

Keepsake boxes: These are great little items for decorating
with the motif, as they are usually anything but plain and
are kept within view. Moreover, the target is likely to handle the box and come into direct contact with your curse
as items are placed inside or perused.

Scrapbook or photo album cover: As with the keepsake
box, these items are handled by the target regularly as he or
she creates pages and adds pictures.

Planter: If the subject of your intent is a plant person, this
is the ideal gift. Just make sure to seal the curse so that it
doesn't include the plant.

Sun catcher: If you're a stained glass artisan or like to work
with the colored plastic resins that emulate the medium,
give this a shot. Folks love a sun catcher and will hang it up
immediately.

Wall hanging, eyeglass case, Tarot bag: These are excellent
items to make and gift if you aren't clumsy with a needle
but don't want to invest the time it takes to make a quilt.
And as they'll be used constantly, the nine-patch will definitely have occasion to do its job.

Stitches that Bring Nervous Twitches

Stitchery—from that wielded by the gown-designing mice in *Cinderella* to the tapestry-stitching women in *The Mists of Avalon*—has long been depicted as a source of magic and spell-craft. But only in books and movies, you say. Not so. Having been raised in the deep South where all female children are taught the arts of the needle as soon as they can hold one, I can assure you that there's more to it than simple entertainment. You see, I grew up in a time when embroidered samplers, linens, and dish towels were out of style, nobody would have dreamed of wearing darned socks, and it was completely unnecessary to sew one's own clothes. And yet, we were required to practice our stitches every day.

Of course, no one ever told us specifically that stitchery was magical. But somehow, we knew. Maybe it was the fact that—at that time, at least—it was reserved only for ladies. Maybe it was the fact that, even if we had more to do than we could handle, nothing—not plague, nor fire, nor the appearance of the Four Horsemen, Themselves—ever got in the way of that stitching hour after lunch. But I suspect it was something else entirely: It was in the care we learned to take in the planning phase, choosing just the right designs, just the right stitches, and just the right colors to make each piece our very own. And when you're taught that the planning is more important than the actual stitching . . . well . . . there's got to be a reason.

I was well into my teens before I purposely imbued a stitchery project with magic, and the results were so astounding that I've never again stitched anything without. But how could the results have been otherwise? Since stitches, themselves, are inherently magical—with each having its own strengths, its own energies, and its own functions—actively imbuing any project with magic only serves to strengthen its mission.

That's all well and fine. But what does stitchery have to do with this particular subject matter? More to the point, how can it be used to that end?

As with everything else in life, individual stitches have both passive and aggressive tendencies. This means that they can be used for any sort of magic, regardless of the desired outcome. And in the case of hexes, curses, and other unsavory magic, it's just a matter of examining the stitches in question, looking at their symbolisms, and seeing which will suit your purpose. It's as easy as that.

One of the best things about using stitches, though, nearly goes without saying: The possibilities for incorporating them into magic are positively limitless. You can showcase them or hide them. You can use them in embroidery and sewing projects, add them to handkerchiefs and scarves, sweaters, blouses, and pants, and include them unseen in the linings of pockets. You can even incorporate them in greeting cards, if the stock is heavy enough. The list goes on and on.

While nearly any stitch can be employed within a hex or curse or other magical manipulation, the space here doesn't allow for a comprehensive list. For your convenience, however, a few of my favorites and their purposes are included below. For more ideas, check out your public library or local bookstore. There is a multitude of wonderful stitchery books on the market, and any one of them will spur your creativity.

Running stitches: Stitched crookedly, these stitches will keep your target from staying the course and cause him or her to meander from one thing to another. Stitch them in a straight line to keep the errant lover on the straight and narrow.

French knots: Use these to foul up your target's efforts and keep goals from being accomplished. They also work well in efforts where putting an end to undesirable behavior is the goal.

Chain stitch: Try these to impart continual misery with a domino effect. They can also be used to set a chain of events into motion, with each stitch representing one of the events.

Cross stitch: Since X marks the spot, these are perfect for any type of hex or curse. These stitches can also be used to bind two people together.

Feather stitch: Use this stitch to destroy focus, scatter energy, and force the target to take on more than is humanly possible. And because it creates "dead ends," it's also useful when your goal is to send your target on a wild goose chase or cause his or her every effort to come to naught.

Herringbone stitch: Because this stitch resembles a split-rail fence, it's perfect for fencing your target in and blocking desires from coming to fruition.

Disturbing the Peace
with the Dream Police

Today's world is so busy that just doing our jobs isn't enough. Instead, we're forced to multi-task, expected to produce more than ever, and required to jump on the treadmill of over-achievement. We race to work and juggle appointments, meetings, and a ton of other things that David Copperfield couldn't manage on his best day. And then we race toward home. But that's no better. We have laundry to do, grocery lists to fill, and family activities to coordinate. And when we're finally done—often in the wee hours of the morning—we're so exhausted that all we can think about is falling into bed and catching a few hours of sleep.

Taking all this into account, it's little wonder that the bed has become absolute refuge for most of us. It's the one place where we don't have to check off a to-do list, where we're immune to the barking of orders, and where we're safe from everything, including performance evaluation. It's the one place where we can sink into oblivion and embrace the peace that nothing else provides. And because it's the one place where nothing other than simple existence is expected of us, we've come to treasure that sanctuary and the restful sleep associated with it. In fact, we'd do nearly anything to protect it.

Perhaps that's why dream catchers have become such a popular gift-giving idea and why the recipients, whether they truly believe in the tool's power or not, never fail to hang them up immediately. It's also why curses connected with these fabulous little devices work so well.

While the dream catcher normally works to keep bad dreams out and allow pleasant ones to flow through, such is not the case with those prepared for cursing. In fact, the exact opposite is true. Not only do nightmares flow through to the dream world and plague the target, but the horrors involved showcase you and the harm that he or she has caused you. The target wakes in a cold sweat—heart pounding, hands shaking, and head aching—with neither respite nor escape until amends are made.

Of course, a ready-made dream catcher probably won't accomplish this—at least, not fully. You'll have to make one yourself; so the webbing is woven in a counter-clockwise fashion, and the curse is worked in from the beginning. But not to worry. A dream catcher is easy to make, and complete instructions can be found in the spell section of Part Two.

Wicked Witchin' in the Kitchen

While hexes and curses can certainly be stirred into food, doing so can be downright dangerous. And because of that, I nearly excluded this section from the book. The problem is fairly obvious: You never know who might take a bite of that accursed casserole, and the last thing you want is for a child, a pet, or some innocent person to inadvertently consume the just desserts you've just whipped up for your target. None of us would want to be responsible for that.

Excluding it, though, presented another problem. As a kitchen Witch, I know that some of the most powerful magic known to humankind comes directly from the kitchen. Why? Because the kitchen is the heart of the home. It symbolizes our very sustenance. Further, we form strong emotional attach-ments to the aromas that emanate from that room—emotional attachments that linger in its very atmosphere—the sort of emotional attachments that can be used to fuel our very magic.

If that alone weren't a good enough reason to include the information, there's this: What better way to send magical effects directly to a target than through ingestion and forcing the two to become one? There is none. And because of that, I simply couldn't write this book without it.

How to include the information responsibly, though, took some thought. So, what you'll find here really doesn't fit the hexes and curses category. (If you want to go there, that's fine. But know that you're on your own.) Instead, it more closely resembles those "unsavory notions" mentioned in this book's subtitle. And what does that mean exactly? Precisely what the words imply. You'll find interesting tidbits related to keeping that errant lover at home, breaking up a relationship, and cre-ating a case of lust so hot that nothing in this world could begin to cool it. Loosening your partner's hold on the bank accounts more your style? You'll find that too, as well as ways to get what you want when you want it, regardless of who or what is currently standing in your way. It's all very handy information to have at your fingertips and much more fun than risking an innocent party's demise.

Stirring the Pot

It never fails to amaze me just how many cooking-related things we do in the kitchen that we simply take for granted. We don't know where they came from or why we do them. There's certainly no thought at all to their magical significance. And yet, we know that most every action has at least one.

Take adding grains of rice to our salt shakers, for example. While the rice does, indeed, absorb moisture and keep the salt from crystallizing, there's more to it than that. For one thing, it's said that dry salt brings good fortune—since it wards off evil, that makes perfect sense—but that damp salt is an omen of death in the family. Add that to the fact that the magical properties of rice vibrate to abundant blessings, and you have a veritable good-luck spell on your hands.

There's also the fact that we add salt to water we plan to boil. Although most of us think it's a simple matter of bringing water to a boil more quickly, there's more to that, as well. In ancient times, it was added as an offering to the Gods, so They'd bless the contents of the pot and prevent good fortune from escaping with the steam.

That brings us to stirring the pot. And whether right-handed or left-handed, whether working in a circular motion or a figure eight, it's something that everyone involuntarily handles in the same fashion: We all stir clockwise. How does this happen? Well, it's just one of those interesting human phenomena—a phenomenon with a basis in magic. When we stir clockwise, we emulate the movement of the Sun. And in doing so, we reap His blessings—general gain and success, health, wealth, good luck, etc.—not only upon the food we're preparing but upon all those who partake of it.

However, if we choose to stir the pot in a counter-clockwise motion—and this will take some doing as stirring in the other direction is completely automatic—it drastically changes the energies contained within the food. Need proof? When a pot is about to boil over, just point at it, move your finger clockwise around the outside perimeter, and see what happens. The level of the contents lowers in the pot, and there's no need to turn down the heat. That's because you've changed the vibrational energy of the substance. And it's precisely this type of energy that you'll want to accumulate when working extremely manipulative magic and build upon while visualizing your intent.

One other thing: if you're going to use food to accomplish your goals, be absolutely certain that you name your target during preparation. Why? Because you'll want to prevent the magic within the food from affecting you or someone else. In fact, it's a good idea to take things a step further and charge any prepared food with the incantation below. This is one case where it truly is better to be safe than sorry!

Food Enchantment Incantation

The magic that's within this dish
Is meant for (name of target), *as is my wish.*
On others who may hear its call
It shall not have any effect at all.
Pure delight is all they'll feel
As they fill their plates and eat this meal.
But (name of target), *it will hit magically.*
As I will, so mote it be.

Magical Tidbits

The following comprises a few ideas as to what foods and seasonings may be incorporated into meals to accomplish your goals. As you expand upon this list—and you will—just one note of caution: some herbs are poisonous! With that in mind, please check a reliable herbal before incorporating any substance with which you're unfamiliar.

Basil: Season foods with this herb to loosen a partner's hold on the money and force him or her to spend some on you.

Bread braid: As it's pulled apart and consumed, bread baked in this form can be used to separate lovers and break up relationships.

Cayenne pepper: Commonly known as the "hot foot powder of the culinary world," this little gem works wonders when it comes to getting your way. Be sure to apply it liberally.

Cinnamon: Fold and mix this into recipes to induce and secure love. (Pies, rolls, cakes, cookies, and wine are good options.) Sprinkle it on top of beverages to obtain money.

Clove: Long known for its powers of seduction, add ground or powdered clove to hot beverages and desserts to induce lust. (Once you've got the target in the position desired, add it to massage oil to really liven things up!)

Ginger: Add this to foods to increase sexual endurance and stamina.

Kava-Kava root: This peppery-tasting substance induces a natural state of euphoria and relaxes the judgment centers, making them open to suggestion. The key, though, is that it must be fresh or freshly dried. And since it's most effective when added to a butter or milk base, it's the perfect addition to eggnog, cream sauces, or gravies.

Mint: Incorporate to cool anger and force your target to chill out—even if you're the one at fault.

Nuts: Want to plant the seeds of your desires in the target's head and make them think it was their idea? Just add any type of nut to the food you're serving. Nuts may also be used to plant seeds of doubt.

Potato: If a target is standing in the way of what you want, carve his or her initials in a potato, then cut it into small pieces before cooking and serving. (It's also useful to add a dollar sign to the carving if your target is being stingy with money.)

Saltpeter: A pinch of this added to any food will definitely keep any lover from straying. It's important to note, however, that while your lover won't stray, he or she won't be able to perform with you either.

Sesame seeds: Because these are sacred to both Ganesha and Hecate, they are excellent additions when used to remove obstacles and get what you want.

The Gift That Keeps on Giving

While most curses are designed to do their jobs and dissipate, upon occasion we have need of one that goes a little further. Sometimes, we need it to work indefinitely. And when those times arise, a little bit of aggravation simply isn't going to do the trick. We need something that, like the Energizer Bunny, keeps on going. And it's on those occasions that it's best to give a gift—a gift like no other—a gift that has a curse built right in.

Of course, not just any gift will do. It's going to have to be something that the subject of your intent is going to be delighted with and will love beyond all reason. Otherwise, it will just get tossed aside or thrown away, and all your efforts will be for naught.

Admittedly, this may be the most difficult thing you've ever done—especially since it requires you to purchase something absolutely lovely for your least favorite person in the world. However, there are reasons that you may actually want to go this route. And it's those reasons that will keep you smiling all the way to the checkout line.

What sort of reasons? Well, for one thing, your target is going to feel guilty as hell for having done you dirty if you turn up with a nice gift—and that, in itself, is part of the curse. Every time he or she looks at that gift or uses it, a vision of you and how you were treated will be the first thing to surface in the mind's eye. And that's exactly why it's important that the person not be able to part with the gift.

Another reason for handling things in this fashion is that while you can certainly weave any curse you'd like into the object, your personal energy is not attached to it in the same way it would be if you crafted the gift yourself. And this not only disassociates you somewhat from the target but helps to keep some of that negative residue at bay.

If that's not enough to convince you, there's this: Your target will never suspect that you are in any way responsible for the sudden turn that his or her life has taken. You did, after all, knock yourself out to obtain that wonderful gift. And anyone who goes to all that trouble couldn't be anything but kind, compassionate, loving, and gracious. Right?

Taking this avenue is easy once you get past having to purchase the gift. There are, however, a few rules of thumb. Do yourself a favor, follow them carefully, and those worrisome afterthoughts won't come to call.

- **Do not involve living creatures.** I shouldn't have to spell this out, but I will just to ease my own mind. This means absolutely no plants or animals.

- **Only purchase gifts suitable for adults.** This means no stuffed animals, no dolls, or any other toy that might inadvertently fall into the hands of a child or a pet.

- **In the case of music boxes, be mindful of the tune.** While the music may be uplifting, it should not, in any way, empower the target. A box that plays "*When You Wish Upon a Star,*" for example, is a magical no-no.

Mind Games

Some of you already know that my ex-husband was having an affair with our next-door neighbor. And those of you who have attended my Swifting of Energy seminar know exactly when that knowledge came to light in such a way that I could no longer deny it. What most of you don't know, however, is that I'd delivered a curse upon the two of them long before I was completely enlightened—a curse that also included those who were actively involved in helping them perpetuate the affair and hide the truth, and caused everyone concerned a great amount of difficulty.

Oh, it was the curse to end all curses, all right. And the end results were much stronger than I'd ever dreamed. In fact, the word "difficulty" doesn't even begin to describe them. One man lost his wife, his family, his business, and his home. The ex-husband lost his nerve, his job, and all capacity for reasonable decision-making. And the girlfriend? Well . . . after attempting to commit suicide several times, she wound up getting exactly what she thought she wanted: My ex. But he wasn't at all the prize she'd imagined. Unfortunately for her, he turned out to be a liar, a cheat, and a thief. Even worse, he refused to have her in his life unless she gave up the most precious gift she'd ever had: her only child. And since she actually did that rather than turn her back and walk away, I guess it could be said that she lost her mind as well.

So, what did I do to effect all that mess? Well . . . I can assure you that it wasn't as involved as you might think. Nor did I intend for it to work as it did. It just goes to prove that the power of the mind—all alone and without any magical accoutrements whatsoever—is much more potent than we could possibly imagine.

It all started innocently enough, or so it appeared. The husband and his best friend were going hunting for the weekend, and during hunting season, that was a normal course of events in our household. So, I did what I normally did. I cleaned the camper, stocked it with groceries, made sure the bedding was clean, and packed his clothes and gear for the weekend. I kissed him goodbye as he left and went on about my business.

All went well until a few hours later when I realized that my neighbor hadn't come home from work. And then, I remembered something. She'd packed her car to the brim with luggage and all sorts of other stuff before she'd left that morning. And suddenly, it hit me: The woman next door was on that hunting trip too, and I knew beyond a shadow of a doubt that it was my then-husband she'd gone to meet.

Well . . . I didn't just see red. I saw the most brilliant shade of scarlet known to the color wheel. And then I got down-right pissed. I romped and stomped, screamed and yelled. I paced through the house until I'd worn serious tracks in the carpet and repeatedly called his mobile phone to no avail until the numbers on my telephone keypad were completely illegible. Then I worked myself into one hell of a tizzy. And when I was done with that, I threw the biggest hissy fit ever known to humankind. By the time I was finished, that "hell hath no fury" line that's so often associated with angry women didn't even begin to describe my state of mind. I was out for blood. And I intended to have, at the very least, a figurative bucket full.

Yes, I'd decided to go out to the hunting site and irrevocably reinvent their personal realities. But as I stomped my way to the door, something changed my mind. You see, even though the day had been calm and clear, the sky had suddenly turned dark. The winds began to blow. And as it twirled through the leaves, I relaxed. As it picked up force, I smiled. And when at last, it began to howl that incessant howl that scares the hell out of small children and sends wildlife scurrying for cover, I did what any other Witch in my position would do: I laughed right out loud.

Truth be told, I've always been somewhat of a weather mage. But my real talent—if you could call it that—has always been in transferring the force of my displeasure into storm creation. And since I'd already managed to brew one up, there was certainly no point in letting it going to waste. So, I talked to the winds. I talked to the clouds. I talked to the sky and the rain and the lightning. And when I was sure all were well on their way to the hunting site, I talked some more. Only this time, it was to Kali—one of my Patronesses—best known for Her role in absolute destruction.

Now usually, I'm not an advocate of leaving anything up to the Universe, the Deities, or anything else. So why I did it that night is still unclear to me. But after listing my grievances, I told Her that I wanted the ultimate revenge and that I wanted their world rocked and set on end. But most of all, I wanted them to be forced to eat their just desserts. Not just once, mind you. But over and over and over again until they literally gagged at the thought of having to take one more bite. And I finished up by saying that I didn't give a damn how She made it happen as long as it happened posthaste and the results were very miserable and extremely long-lasting.

Well, I got what I asked for, all right. And an early morning phone call delivered the news. My then-husband and his buddy, David, had cut their outing short—a severe storm had seen to that—and were on their way back to town. Furthermore, they wanted to take me to breakfast.

Of course, I was dying to find out what had happened, but to mention it might have meant giving myself away. So, we were halfway through our meal when David finally demanded to know just exactly where I'd been the night before.

"At home," I said, meeting his gaze directly. "Where else would I have been?"

He stared at me from across the table, his face a picture of disbelief.

"I don't know," he finally answered. "But some really weird stuff happened last night. And the only time I've ever seen that much crap happen in one place at one time was when you were . . . well . . . when you were . . . "

I cocked an eyebrow and smiled at him sweetly, innocently, and as if I had no clue in the world as to what he might be referring to "When I was what, David?"

"Well . . . when you were . . . involved!"

Apparently, the night had been a complete disaster. The storm had rocked the camper unmercifully; so much so, in fact, that nobody had been able to sleep a wink. But that wasn't the worst of it. The area had begun to flood, so even though the rain was coming down in sheets, they'd not only had to move camp to higher ground right in the middle of that mess, but they'd had to do it without benefit of light, since their flashlights were all on the blink. No sooner had they gotten set up again than lightning hit a dead tree less than thirty yards from the camper. And if that hadn't been bad enough, the four-wheeler—which had been battened down securely on the trailer—had come to life and taken on a mind of its own. Yes, it had loosened its bonds and rolled off the trailer, made a left, and kept on going until, finally, it ended its midnight journey by climbing up the camper steps and landing with a thud against the front door.

I forced myself to look shocked, but it was all I could do not to jump for joy. For at that point, I realized that Kali had, indeed, begun to serve Her version of just desserts. What better way, after all, to dole out misery than to trap three claustrophobic people in a small pop-up camper with no way to get out and armed only with the knowledge that they'd have to stay in that situation until daybreak?

Of course, I had no idea what form the remainder of their just desserts would take. Nor did I realize just how much retribution there would be. I only knew that the curse was alive, well, and on track. And all that I had to do from that moment on, was sit back, relax, and watch the rest of it manifest.

The Key Ingredient

The fact of the matter is that there is nothing on the face of this Earth—not an oil, a powder, a wash, or even the best planned ritual—that can manufacture or deliver a curse as well as simple mind power. And as there's no physical evidence to point in your direction, there's no better way to hide your tracks either. It's the best possible way to immerse a curse, bar none.

So, why don't more people go this route? The reasons are many, but the most common is that they just don't believe it will work. They think they've got to have the trappings of ritual items to do the job properly. And since successful magic is nine-tenths belief that the intended results will manifest, they're probably right. They're much better off sticking to what they know and handling things within their comfort zones.

Another reason is that they lack focus. How do I know? Because the number of emails I get from folks who can't even manage a simple spell from my book *Everyday Magic* tells the tale. In order for any sort of magic to work, the mind cannot be allowed to wander. It must be totally focused on the task at hand. And sadly enough, most folks simply don't have that sort of attention span.

With enough practice, however, focus can be learned. And once it is, lots of things begin to happen in the personal realm. Self-confidence returns, and with that, the perception of what is possible changes drastically. It becomes much easier to believe that your magical efforts—even those engineered without benefit of ritual props—will not only work, but will work to their full capacity.

The mundane side effects are fabulous too. For once you learn to focus and extend your attention span, you'll discover that most of those normal, day-to-day problems—the ones that drive you crazy on a regular basis—simply cease to exist. And it's all because you've learned to pay attention and follow things through.

So, how exactly do you learn to focus? It's not as difficult as you might think. In fact, the following exercises put me on the right track years ago, and I'm willing to bet that they'll help you too. Just remember to practice often, practice long, and practice hard. If you don't, it's a sure bet that none of the spells in this book are going to work for you as planned. And that would, indeed, be a shame!

The Exercises

Focus Exercise #1

For this exercise, you may either write on paper or use the word-processing program on your computer. (If the latter is your choice, set the program to double-space, and set all the margins—top and bottom, right and left—to one inch.) Now, letting your mind wander, write or type your thoughts just as quickly as you can think them. It doesn't matter if it looks like psychobabble. It doesn't matter if your thoughts don't resemble complete sentences. Just get them down as quickly as you can, and don't stop until you've filled three pages.

Focus Exercise #2

As in the first exercise, you'll either use paper and pen or your computer. Place an object in front of you anything will do, be it an apple, an ashtray, a piece of jewelry, a knickknack, or some other item—and examine it carefully. Now keeping that object in the forefront of your mind, begin to write about it. Start with its color, its shape, its texture, and its lines. Proceed with any specific odor it may exude, then talk about why you have it, what you use it for, how you feel about it, and why you haven't gotten rid of it. Keep going until you've written three pages.

Chapter 5

Dispersing the Curse

While there are definitely times that magic can be delivered successfully without the use of anything but a thought, a look, a
gesture, or maybe a few well-flung words, there are also times
when we know that's just not going to cut it. It's those times
that we reach for the pen and paper and get busy writing a
ritual or spell that we're sure will get the job done. Most of us
start with the incantation since it's the part that seems to take
the longest. We engage in games of wordplay, switch this for
that, and rotate verse and sentence structures to improve the
clarity of meaning and intent. We work at it until we're sure
that even someone with only two brain cells to rub together
would understand our meaning and that there's no chance of
error or mistaking what we want.

Then, quite pleased with ourselves since the hard part is
done, we sit back and start to think about what else we'll need
for this ritual. We check our personal reference libraries, make
a list of our choices, and set off to obtain the ritual supplies
that will tie the whole thing together. That, of course, is when a
peculiar look crosses most of our faces. Why? Because we soon
come to realize three very important things.

First, we discover that the items on our lists simply aren't to be had at the local metaphysical shop—at least, not in ready-made form—and even if the store does carry the ingredients for making them ourselves, we don't know what those might be or how to put them together properly. But we're magical practitioners, for Gods' sake; we have a ritual to perform, and we're not to be deterred. So we take a deep breath, march up to the counter, and ask the clerk for advice. And that's when the second very important thing grabs our attention: The folks at the shop are just as clueless as we are. Most of them have never even heard of this stuff, much less have any idea where we might find it. And now, number three begins to dawn bright and clear: We suddenly realize that we were very sadly mistaken. The hard part isn't done at all. In fact, it's just beginning.

So, now what? Do we scrap the ritual and that lovely incantation? Do we use the incantation anyway and hope like hell it's powerful enough to stand on its own? Or do we continue to search for these items until we're so old and decrepit that we can remember neither why we wanted them in the first place nor why we even cared?

Absolutely not. Help is on the way—and it's right here in this chapter.

True enough, the items often associated with hexing and its antidote tend to have rather odd names—Goofer Dust, Hot Foot Powder, Four Thieves Vinegar, and so on—but the actual ingredients that comprise them aren't strange at all. In fact, I'm willing to bet that you've got most of what you need already, right there in your kitchen cabinets. It's usually just a matter of having the recipes at hand and knowing what to do with the finished product, both of which I've included here.

Occasionally though, there will be that ingredient or two that not only seems to be essential to the concoction at hand, but also completely evades all attempts at reasonable capture. So, I've done my best to rectify that problem as well by playing with the recipes until I found substitutions that don't hamper strength or effectiveness, and will be fairly easy to locate.

As the Cauldron Bubbles . . .

With the major problems solved, let's talk a little bit about the recipes. The first thing you'll probably notice is that the proportions aren't listed in most of them. But there's good reason for that. It simply means that unless otherwise noted, you should start out with equal portions of each ingredient. And since you're not likely to be mixing up large amounts of any one substance—at least not right away—I suggest you begin with a teaspoon of each. Then later, if you discover that you're using more of a particular product, you can always increase the amounts and make a larger batch.

It's also important to mention that, unless noted otherwise, all of the recipes that follow are versatile as far as form. This means that the ingredients in an incense recipe can also be blended as an oil, a powder recipe can be used to mix a wash, and so forth. (The only exceptions are Eviction Notice Powder and Swamp Water.) There are, however, a few tricks I've picked up over the years when it comes to working with particular supply forms. And to save you time and trouble, I've included them below.

Preparation Tips

Incense Tips

If you don't plan to burn the incense on charcoal, you'll have to add an incense base to your recipe. While some stores carry incense base and have it available for purchase, I've also discovered that sawdust works well, as do small twigs pulverized in a coffee grinder. A pinch of saltpeter will also do the trick. But if you go that route, be absolutely certain to only use a pinch. Otherwise, your ritual may have to be amended to include an evocation to the local fire department!

Just an aside: While the incense you've just mixed may smell heavenly, know that it doesn't always smell as good when burning. In fact, some of these recipes may not smell good at all. And if that's the case, just remember that you're using it for a HIP—a hex in progress—and nothing about a hex is lovely except the end result: that point where your foe stops screwing with you!

If you're using a coffee grinder and you're preparing several different mixtures, it's important to clean the grinder between uses. Start by scrubbing it with a brush and a 50:50 mixture of rubbing alcohol and water—this will break down any resin residue—then follow with hot, soapy water, and finish with a boiling water rinse.

Oil Tips

Always try to find your ingredient list already in oil form. Then using an eyedropper and a clean bottle, blend two drops of each oil together at a time. Increase by one drop each until you have enough of the finished product to do the current job. In this way, you'll keep the original oils intact and have them on hand for other uses.

If you must use dry ingredients for oil-making, use a base oil that doesn't turn rancid. (Grape-seed or jojoba oils are good choices.) Place the dry ingredients in an electric potpourri pot, and mash them up with a fork to bruise them. Pour in just enough oil to cover, then turn on the pot. Heat for twelve hours, stirring every two to three hours, adding a bit more oil if necessary. Strain, bottle, and use. (Please note that while the oil may not have much fragrance at this point, the aroma—or lack thereof—has no bearing on magical potency.)

While it's certainly okay to reuse bottles, be absolutely sure they're clean before using them to blend anything else. (The last thing you want is the residue of an opposing concoction mixed with the new blend.) Wash them in hot, soapy water to which you've added a little bleach, then scrub the insides thoroughly with a small bottle brush. Scald them with boiling water after, or put them in the dishwasher for a full cycle.

Powder Tips

When preparing a powder, you'll want to grind the ingredients as finely as possible. While you can accomplish this with a mortar and pestle, I've found that it's much easier to toss the ingredients into a coffee grinder, set it to "fine," and hit the button. (You may have to do this two or three times.)

To give this mixture a powder-like consistency, stir in a teaspoon or two of cornstarch before using.

Clean the coffee grinder between uses following the directions outlined previously for Incense Tips.

Wash Tips

There's nothing like an automatic drip coffeemaker when it comes to brewing washes. Just put a filter in the filter cup, add the ingredients, fill, and brew. Then add the mixture to a gallon of water. (Note: Since some of your ingredients may be poisonous, do NOT use your regular coffeemaker for this purpose. Obtain an inexpensive one—thrift stores and yard sales are good starting points—and use it instead.)

Before you brew again, clean both the filter cup and pot thoroughly, following the directions above for Oil Tips.

What Form to Fix to Aid the Tricks

Before we get to the recipes, it's important to decide what form of the product actually suits your needs best. If your curse actually involves paying a visit to the target's home, for example, then a powder or wash may be just the thing. But if it doesn't, an oil or incense may be more appropriate. It all depends on the curse at hand and how you plan to deliver it.

Deliver it?

You hadn't thought about that, had you?

If your answer is no, don't feel bad. While curse writing and planning generally come easily once folks decide to take that route, it's common for the actual delivery plan to completely slip the mind. That's because we just expect the curse to spring from the altar and deliver itself, and that's not always the case.

Chances are, of course, that you'd rather your subject be oblivious to the fact that you cursed them. And the last thing you want is to be caught at it, which is exactly what could happen if you're ballsy enough to run over to their house in the middle of the night, armed with washes or powders or something to bury on their property. Even worse, you might be arrested for trespassing. And since spending the night in the pokey certainly wouldn't play well into your plans, that's something you'd do well to steer clear of.

This doesn't mean that you can't engineer your curse to deliver itself. Neither does it mean that powders and washes may not be appropriate to your purpose. It simply means that you may have to rework things a bit and take some extra precautions. But if you've already gone to all the trouble of working out the curse at hand, thinking it through again is certainly worth the effort. Especially if it guarantees your success.

That said, the various forms that the recipes can take, as well as the different ways they can be used, are listed below for your convenience. Please note that some of them also list certain precautions. And if you don't want to deal with unsavory residue later, you'd do well to heed them.

Speaking of precautions, there's one other thing that bears mention before we begin. Regardless of the form you decide upon, one thing holds true for all: Clearly visualize your target during preparation, then dispose of any leftovers once the cursing ritual is complete. (Do NOT use on any other subject!) By doing this, you'll safeguard others from harm should they accidentally touch the substance.

Incense

- Burn during cursing ritual.

- Use to smudge the poppet.

- Place inside body cavities of poppet.

- Add to gris gris bags (mojo or charm bags) to strengthen the properties of the other contents. The bag is then hidden on the target's property. Usually, it's buried. But if a coworker is the target, hiding it in their desk drawer or behind their desk is also an option.

Precautions:

After use, clean the coffee grinder as previously directed in the Incense Tips section.

Cleanse your ritual area by smudging it with Uncrossing Incense. (See recipes later in this chapter.)

Oils

- Use to anoint the candle used in cursing ritual.

- Anoint the poppet; or moisten cotton with a few drops, and place inside the appropriate body cavity.

- Rub on your hands, and touch the target to imbue him or her with its properties. (Once this is accomplished, clean your hands thoroughly with rubbing alcohol—alcohol wipes are great for this—and wash your hands with plenty of soap and hot water.)

- Use to anoint a letter or package that you send to the target.

- Give to the target as a present, and get the subject to use it on themselves. (This can be a bit tricky, but telling them that it's a "power oil" works occasionally.)

Precautions:

Cover work area completely with several layers of newspaper, and remove them from your home immediately when work is finished. Alternatively, burn them and dispose of the ashes.

Dispose of any leftovers outside the home.

Clean your hands thoroughly. (See previous instructions under Oils.)

Powders

- Sprinkle across the threshold, porch, or sidewalk of the target's home—or any other place else that he or she might cross on foot.

- Blow into the target's face. (This really isn't a good idea and is only mentioned here for purposes of historical use.)

- Sprinkle in the target's mailbox to bring bills and legal notices and to keep checks from being delivered. (After the anthrax scares, you may want to be careful with this one too.)

- Sprinkle into your coworker's desk drawer, around his or her chair, and/or around the work area.

- Apply to the poppet using a clean paintbrush, or sprinkle into the body cavities. Either discard the paintbrush after use, or clean it thoroughly. (The dishwasher is a good option.)

Precautions:

Cover work area completely with several layers of newspaper, and remove them from your home immediately when work is finished. Alternatively, burn them and dispose of the ashes.

Wear surgical gloves during use, and dispose of them immediately. If household gloves are worn instead, soak them after use in hot bleach water, then place them on the top rack of the dishwasher or in the washing machine for final cleaning.

Flush any leftovers down the toilet or garbage disposal. Follow with plenty of water and the juice of one lemon, then flush with water again.

Pour three tablespoons of salt and the juice of one lemon into a clean spray bottle, then fill it with water and shake well. Use this mixture to clean your work surface, then follow with your favorite household cleaner. (This mixture may be saved for future use.)

Washes

- Spray on front door, porch, sidewalk or any other place the subject might walk. Also may be sprayed into the target's footprint.

- Use to wash the walls, floors, and fixtures of the target's home. While this may seem to be a moot point—just how in the hell are you going to accomplish this?!—it may not be as farfetched as it seems. Depending upon who the target is (a relative, a former friend, an acquaintance, etc.), you may be able to offer cleaning services for a day.

- If the target is a coworker, spray his or her work area or cubicle. Just spraying it as "air freshener" there will do the trick too.

- Apply to the poppet using a clean paintbrush, or add a few drops to cotton and stuff into the body cavities. (If a paintbrush is used, see previous instructions for Powders.)

- Spray on a gris gris bag to seal it with the curse.

- In the case of Swamp Water, use as a poppet disposal tool.

Precautions:
(See precautions for Powders.)

The Recipes

Little aggravates me more than not being able to find what I need when I need it. And this is especially true of magical formulae. (What's worse, after all, than being right in the middle of a magical operation and having to stop midstream to chase down that elusive incense recipe?) To that end, this section is organized in alphabetical order for easy use and look-up. But that's not all. You'll find every formula mentioned in this book—regardless of magical flavor—included here as well. It's one-stop brewing at its best.

Activation Incense

Use this incense in rituals to activate a poppet. It's also a good choice for rituals that initiate any sort of hex.

Ginger
Nutmeg
Black pepper

Bitch Be Gone Powder (Lady Dame's Formula)

According to Lady Dame, all you have to do is sprinkle a bit of this powder in the path of someone you detest, and "the bitch will be gone!"

Rattlesnake bones, crushed (powdered
*   snake shed may be substituted)*
High John the Conqueror root

Chango Oil

Dedicated to Chango, this oil is used by men to draw romantic partners of the female persuasion. When wearing this oil, just a dab will do it, guys!

2 apple seeds
Cinnamon
Coconut
Frankincense
Musk

Commanding/Controlling/Compelling Powder

Excellent for use in assuring that court cases swing your way. For extra oomph, add a bit of High John the Conqueror to the mix.

Allspice
Cinnamon
Clove
Patchouli
Sandalwood

Crossing Oil
(Sometimes known as Black Arts)

Often used to dress candles used in hexes, as well as to anoint poppets and gris gris bags.

Cinnamon
Graveyard dirt (pinch)
Myrrh
Patchouli
Vetivert
Sage

Crossing Oil #2

It's said that this oil is so powerful that you should never mix or apply it unless you truly mean business and that it should only be used in curses involving the nastiest of the nasty.

Bayberry
Cinnamon
Myrrh

Devil Be Gone Powder

Used to break strong curses and hexes, this powder is usually sprinkled on the target as well as around the room and over the altar. Some folks say that "interesting" things happen when this formula is burned as an incense, but I've never found that to be true.

Bay leaf
High John the Conqueror
Hyssop
Lavender
Salt
Vervain

Eviction Notice Powder

This is indispensable when it comes to removing nasty spirits from the home. To seal the home against their return, add a tablespoon to your cleaning water, and use it to scrub floors and baseboards. (Do NOT use as incense!!)

Asafoetida
Gun powder

Fiery Wall of Protection Incense

This is an excellent formula for clearing negative energy from the home. It's important to note, though, that since this incense is largely made of resins, it produces large amounts of smoke.

Dragon's Blood
Frankincense
Myrrh
Salt

Four Thieves Vinegar

While this mixture has many purposes including some that involve good luck, it's often added to other items related to hexes and is said to keep enemies far from your door.

Adam and Eve root
Black pepper
High John the Conqueror
Vetivert
Bottle of apple cider vinegar

Goofer Dust Powder

A good all-purpose hexing powder, always include at least a spoonful when disposing of a poppet.

Graveyard dirt (see Chapter 2)
Patchouli leaves or root

Goofer Dust Powder #2

Black pepper
Cayenne pepper
Graveyard dirt
Wasp's nest or snakeskin, crushed and crumbled

High John the Conqueror Incense

Although generally used for positive purposes such as bringing good luck and health, and attracting money, this recipe is also used to control one's enemies; thus, its place in this section.

High John the Conqueror
Orange peel

Hot Foot Powder

Okay . . . so Hot Foot Powder doesn't really burn the feet. But once someone steps in it, they will make tracks and leave in a hurry. For that reason, it's used to make nasty neighbors move away. (Just sprinkle a little in their yard or close to their front door.) It can also be rubbed on the feet of a poppet to force the target to leave you alone.

Black pepper
Cayenne pepper
Cumin
Salt
Sulfur (2 parts)

Loosen the Purse Powder

While this will work on anyone who's so tight they squeak, it's especially effective on the boss who refuses to give you that well-deserved raise. Just rub some on your hands, touch the greedy bastard, and watch the money flow.

Lavender
Sage
Thyme

Lost and Away Powder

When dealing with folks who can't seem to mind their own business, use this powder to get them out of your life and banish them for good. I'm told that it's also an excellent tool for keeping others from breaking through psychic boundaries.

Crossroads dirt
Mistletoe
Orris
Sage
Sulfur (the heads from three matches work nicely)

Mad Oil (Lady Dame's Formula)

Use this oil when absolute fury is necessary for an effort, and hurt feelings are all you can muster.

Chango oil (if you are male)
High John the Conqueror oil
Oshun oil (if you are female)
Patchouli oil
Rose geranium oil

Murv's Swamp Water Wash

Called Swamp Water because the main ingredient in aspirin comes from the willow tree, this substance is most used in poppet disposal as it literally eats away at the doll, thus eating away at the problems caused by the target.

1 large bottle of aspirin
1 quart of water

Oshun Oil

Dedicated to the Goddess of the same name, this oil is used by women not only to draw love and money but also as a protection from enemies as well. To stay on the good side of Oshun, always taste the honey before adding it, so She knows it isn't poisoned.

Anise
Cinnamon
Honey (a drop or two will do it)
Jasmine
Orange peel
Rose

Peaceful Home Powder

Widely used for uncrossing and generally sprinkled on carpets, this powder literally lifts nasties from their hiding places where they can simply be vacuumed up and disposed of.

Lavender
Lemon peel, dried
Rose petals
Thyme

Queen Bitch of the Whole F***ing Universe Incense
(Also known as Devil's Master)

When it's imperative that others do your bidding—this includes spirits as well as the living—there's little else that does the trick as well.

Chili powder
Cinnamon
Red sandalwood (substitute white sandalwood if necessary)

Separation Powder

Use when your need involves splitting up any sort of relationship, association, or alliance. (Lovers, business partners, and friendships come to mind here.) It can also be used as an incense for poppet-smudging.

Black pepper
Chili powder
Cinnamon
Galangal
Iron filings (rust scrapings may be substituted)
Vetivert

Tall Tale Powder

To force someone to tell the truth, rub a bit on your hands and touch the offending party.

Mint
Nutmeg
Rose petals

Turn Around Incense

Used to smudge the poppet of a target who's betrayed your confidence, this can straighten out the mess he or she has caused and turn your luck around.

Bayberry
Cigarette or pipe tobacco
Goldenseal

Uncrossing Incense

Use in rituals performed for the express purpose of reversing a hex or a curse, or to remove one from yourself.

Bay leaf
Lavender
Rose petals
Sandalwood
Verbena

Van Van Wash

Typically used to bring good fortune into the home, this mixture is also occasionally applied after uncrossing rituals.

Juice of 1 lemon (for other forms, use 1 tablespoon lemon peel)
Rose petals
1 teaspoon vanilla extract (for other forms, use 1 tonka bean)

War Water

Usually tossed in the target's front yard or on his or her property, this substance is also used to sprinkle poppets and gris gris bags.

Add all ingredients to vodka and steep for one week. Then strain and add mixture to one gallon of water.

Pint of Vodka
Black pepper
Iron filings or rusty nails
Lavender
Peel of 1 lemon
Peel of 1 orange
Red pepper
Whole cloves

Wear Away Powder

This does just what the name implies: It wears away the confidence of the target and replaces it with stress, anxiety, and needless worry.

> *Black pepper*
> *Castor bean*
> *Thyme*

Life Is Messy: Clean It Up

If you've followed the instructions and fully visualized your target while concocting and applying the recipes above, you should feel fine. But remember that psychic residue we talked about in Chapter 1? Well, once in a while, some of that will cling to you during the mixing or application stages anyway. And while symptoms vary from person to person, it's usually the blahs that hit first. Sometimes there's nothing more than that, but occasionally other aggravations will come to call. Common side effects include minor bouts of depression, a sudden inability to concentrate, or a state of complete and utter nonproductiveness. And if you begin to experience any of those, the only solution is to get that junk off of you immediately. If you don't, I can nearly guarantee time spent in bed nursing a cold, the flu, or worse.

Fortunately, the remedy is painless, tasteless, pleasurable, and inexpensive. It involves nothing more than taking a bath. And since you probably already take a shower or bath at least once every day, nothing could be easier.

Granted, this isn't exactly your normal sort of bath, as you'll need to be clean before you jump in. It's also going to be necessary to completely immerse yourself in the water several times, hair and all. And because your skin and hair must be allowed to dry naturally, you won't be able to towel off. When compared to the possibility of having to ingest some foul-tasting medicinal concoction, though, that's a pretty small price to pay—especially considering how much better you're going to feel.

There are several different types of baths that will handle the problem quickly and efficiently, and the instructions for all follow below. Each works equally well, so just choose the one that most appeals to you and call it good. You'll be glad you did.

General Instructions for All Baths

Once the bath is ready, sit in the tub, and completely immerse yourself seven times, allowing the mixture to flow into all body openings. (Swish it around in your mouth as well, but do not swallow it.) Stay in the tub for seven minutes, then get out, allowing the moisture on your body and hair to dry naturally.

The Beer Bath

This is a great little psychic cleanser with added perks: it relieves mild depression and is actually good for your skin and hair.

1 12 ounce can of beer
1 tablespoon salt

Add the beer and salt to a warm tub of water. Using your index finger, stir the water clockwise until thoroughly mixed.

The Vinegar Bath

Long known for its healing and curative properties, vinegar also has the capacity to slice through psychic grime, making it perfect for this bath.

1 cup apple cider vinegar
1 tablespoon salt

Add the ingredients to a warm tub of water, then stir clockwise with your index finger until well mixed.

The Uncrossing Bath

If you've got more to worry about than a mild case of the blahs, this is an excellent bath to utilize as it also tends to increase focus and personal productivity.

1 tablespoon lavender flowers, dried
1 tablespoon rose petals, dried
1 tablespoon salt
1 bay leaf
Juice of 1 lemon

Place the dry ingredients in the filter cup of an automatic drip coffeemaker, add a full pot of water, and allow to brew. Mix in the lemon juice, and add the contents to a tub of warm water.

Alternative Cleansing

One of the perks of relaying psychic cleansing instructions in written form is that I don't have to listen to folks debate the pros and cons of the shower versus the bath—at least, not up close and personal. But the downside is that, whether I can actually hear you or not, I know that some of you aren't comfortable with soaking in the tub at all. I know that some of you are already whining and working yourselves up to full-blown bellyaching. But more to the point, I know that some of you are sitting there, book in hand, racking your brains for an alternative solution.

Are you one of those people? If so, you're wasting your time.

Regardless of how you feel about using the bathtub, it truly is the most effective tool when it comes to psychic cleansing. In this case, it provides a means for complete saturation, a thorough cleansing of the body openings, and does so in a time-efficient manner. There is simply no better way to handle the process. But just to be sure that we don't have one of those silly misunderstandings, I'll make this perfectly clear: *if you have a bathtub at your disposal, use it!*

With that out of the way, there are solutions for those of you who live in homes equipped with nothing but a shower. And while those solutions are certainly workable, they're going to take a lot more doing. This means that you're going to have to restructure the recipes, gather a few more tools, and increase your time in the shower to at least thirty minutes. What's more, you're going to have to pay strict attention to detail. Suffice it to say that this won't be the most relaxing shower you've ever taken. But it can still be the most therapeutic if you follow the steps below carefully.

Gather supplies. In addition to the bath ingredients, you'll also need a one-gallon container marked with seven equal portions, a five-gallon bucket, and an empty spray bottle.

Select a bath from the list above and alter the recipe. As you'll have less water for dilution purposes, use only half of the recipe. Just divide the amount of each ingredient by two. In the case of one tablespoon, use a measurement of one and a half teaspoons. (If you opt for the beer bath, it's okay to use the whole can of beer.)

Prepare the recipe. Pour the mixture into the one-gallon container, and fill with warm water. Fill the spray bottle from the container. Pour any remaining solution from the first measurement into the bucket. Then take all the containers to the bathroom and get into the shower.

Spritz. Use the solution in the spray bottle to completely cleanse all body openings. (Instead of squirting the solution into your eyes, apply it with your fingers.) Add any solution left in the bottle to the bucket.

Bathe. Now fill the bucket to the brim with warm water, and pour the contents over your head. Add the next solution measurement from the one-gallon container to the bucket, fill it with warm water, and repeat. Continue the process until all the solution is gone and you've poured seven full buckets of the mixture over your head. Allow your hair and skin to dry naturally.

Chapter 6

Reversing the Curse and Vexing the Hex

I looked at the cards and studied their positions again. There was a problem, all right, but nothing that couldn't be fixed. It was more like a temporary roadblock: something that the client should meet head on and obliterate, but at worst could manage to bypass. And that's exactly what I told the woman sitting in front of me.

"But you don't understand," she wailed. "That other reader said I had a curse on me . . . a really bad one . . . and . . . "

"Oh, come now, Darlin'," I said, putting on my brightest smile and trying to lighten the situation, "I don't see anything like that here. In fact . . . "

"Well, she *did!* And I can't afford to give her five hundred bucks to take it off. I don't *have* five hundred bucks! I don't have . . . " Her voice trailed off as she swiped furiously at the errant tears spilling down her face.

I handed her a tissue and sighed disgustedly. I'd heard this story before—more times than I cared to recall. It was the oldest scam in the book. The one that charlatans pulled on unsuspecting clients who'd just come in for a good time and a little entertainment. By the time the clients left, though, they'd had neither. Instead, they were so terrified at the thought of a life of bad luck that they'd do anything not to have to live through it. Even turn over their bank accounts if that's what it took. And before it was said and done, that's what usually occurred.

It all started out with this manufactured curse. The reader in question would harp on it and harp on it until the client's better judgment took flight and soared right into oblivion. It didn't matter how happy the client actually was—or had been before she'd stepped through the door—she'd suddenly begin to second-guess herself and look for problems that didn't exist. (Surely her husband hadn't sent her flowers because he loved her. No, he must be screwing around. And the help Sally had given her with that project at work? That was just crap too. What Sally really intended to do was tell the boss that she was incapable of doing her own work and get her fired.) And once she started twisting things around in her mind, the result went way beyond a conclusion that life wasn't as wonderful as she'd originally thought. It culminated in total agreement with the reader: she was cursed, and nothing she did would ever turn out right until that horrible, slimy mess that clung to her was once and for all removed.

Now charlatans may be lots of things, but fools, they're not. They read people well. And once they see the client searching her mind for confirmation of these manufactured problems, they swiftly transform themselves into the most caring human beings on the planet. They take the client's hand, pat it gently, and tell her not to worry. They wipe tears and say that everything will be just fine. Sometimes, they even go as far as to offer the client a cup of tea or coffee. Then when things have settled down somewhat and they're sure they have the client's trust, they move in for the kill. They go on to say that they can fix this problem quickly and easily, and all it will take—are you ready for this?!—is the burning of ten specially prepared candles at fifty bucks a pop. A very small price to pay, they say. What, after all, is a lifetime of happiness worth?

Of course, it doesn't stop there. Now that the client's been reeled in and written the check, one of two things happens: either there's routine "maintenance" to prevent future curses, or more episodes of cursing pop up along the way. But it doesn't much matter which route the charlatan takes. Either way, the client keeps writing the checks and the reader is set for life.

I sat back in my chair, waited for my client to compose herself, and surveyed the cards again. Two things became glaringly apparent: first, the blockage I saw had to do with this other reader and the fear she'd instilled, and second, there was no way I was going to persuade this woman to effectively bypass it by ignoring the charlatan's advice. No, I was going to have to do something about it myself. I just prayed that I was as convincing as the person who'd started this whole mess.

"I can help you," I said, looking the woman directly in the eye, "and it won't . . . "

"But I already *told* you! I don't *have* any money. I can't *get* any money. There's no *way* . . . "

I cut her off with a wave of my hand. "And it won't cost you a thing. Unless, of course, you need candles," I added with a chuckle. "And then, I think a buck fifty ought to do it."

She looked at me askance. "You're kidding."

A quick search of my face told her I wasn't. And for the first time since she'd taken the chair across from me, my client actually smiled.

Sometimes you have to pull out the big guns, and that's exactly what I did for my client. But before you wrack your brains to figure out if you've missed something, I can assure you that you haven't. The curse the other reader spoke of was, indeed, manufactured. It was only a ruse to filch my client out of her life savings. And yet, I not only gave her the strongest hex-breaking weapon in my repertoire, I insisted that she use it. What's up with that?

She needed it. Plain and simple.

Here's the deal. As we discussed in Chapter 1, we are often our own worst enemies. We work ourselves up into tizzies, and instead of throwing the hissy fit that would bring such nonsense to a screeching halt, we give our minds free rein. They twirl round and round, searching for inconsistencies, inventing them where there are none, and gathering panic. Before all's said and done, anxiety sets in, paranoia comes to call, and terror rears its ugly head. We become little more than blithering idiots incapable of so much as getting out of bed for fear that this horrible hex—manufactured or not—will find us, harm us, and ruin our lives forever.

If that's not a curse, I don't know what is.

Yet, that's exactly what had happened to my client. And the fact that she'd invented this mess herself didn't make it any less viable. In this case, perhaps, it was even more so, as it was fueled by the power of suggestion at the hands of someone who was supposed to know what she was doing. So, to help this woman, I had to give her the tools to break this self-imposed curse once and for all. Otherwise, she'd have never been able to get on with her life or live it with some semblance of happiness. And finding a way to retrieve that happiness was the real reason she'd come to see me in the first place.

A Little Lesson in Energy

Before we get into this fabulous hex-breaker of mine, we need to talk a little about energy: what it is, what it isn't, and how to use it to its best advantage. You say you already know about energy? Well, before you skip ahead, I urge you to hear me out. Otherwise, the spell isn't going to do you a bit of good, you'll think I've given you a dud, and nothing could be further from the truth.

While we all think we know everything there is to know about energy, most of us are sadly mistaken. Oh, most of us know what it feels like. We even know when it's shifted. And a good number of us know how to direct it. It's just that most of today's magical teachers are negligent when it comes to teaching the basics. If they weren't, we'd never even consider returning negative energy to its sender. And since most of us are perfectly willing to go that route, it's obvious that something's missing. Something that no practitioner can do without. That something is, of course, a thorough understanding of energy and its most basic properties.

To start with, everything—whether it's a doll, or a stone, or a building in your neighborhood—is entirely comprised of energy. And as magical practitioners, all we do is move and direct that substance. It's pretty basic stuff, which most of us already know.

It's what many practitioners don't know about this substance that seems to cause a problem. First of all, energy is just that. It's energy. There's nothing "good" or "bad" about it. It's not dark or light, positive or negative. It's simply a living, breathing force that vibrates to unlimited form and shape.

This isn't to say, however, that some energies don't feel different from others. They do. But it has nothing to do with the energy itself. Instead, it's the practitioner directing the energy who flavors the way it feels.

A better way to explain this might be to take a look at the pixels in a computer graphic. They are only dots of color—nothing more, nothing less. But when an artist moves them together in a particular order and directs them into a proper measurement, an image forms. The pixels, themselves, have no control over whether the image is dreadful and gloomy, or bright and cheerful. They are, after all, just dots of color. It is the artist who brings the image to light—and evokes the desired feeling from those who view it—by moving and directing the pixels in a certain fashion. The same is true of energy and the practitioner.

The other important thing to understand about energy is that it never really goes away. It never dissolves. It never dissipates. In fact, energy is probably the only thing in this world that is truly boundless and everlasting. And that being the case, it only changes shape and form.

Having learned this early on, you can imagine my reaction when someone else's teacher announced that negative energy should always be returned to the sender. I was stunned. Bewildered. And more than just a little appalled. In fact, try as I might, I just couldn't keep my mouth shut.

"But that's just an effort in futility," I blurted out, "and it's certainly not going to fix the problem!"

It was the teacher's turn to be stunned, bewildered, and more than a little appalled.

"And just why not?" she retorted.

"Because if both practitioners have their shields in place—and they certainly should if they're worth their salt—all this is going to do is cause a game of psychic volleyball. The energy's just going to bounce back and forth until someone gets tired. And we can only hope that *someone* is the practitioner who sent the energy in the first place."

Apparently, this had never occurred to the teacher. She'd simply been relaying information passed on from her teachers and truly hadn't given the matter much thought. At any rate, her annoyance had now given way to interest, and she inquired about the solution.

I explained that all energy—regardless of how it feels—is a gift. It's the very substance from which everything is created. And that being the case, it should never be sent back. Instead, it should be grabbed up, moved and directed, and formed and shaped into something entirely different—something wonderful—something that could be used for personal benefit.

A smile crossed the teacher's lips, and then she began to laugh out loud. She wasn't laughing at the solution, though. Instead, it was the irony of the situation. To take someone's ill-will and transform it into something personally beneficial was just plain wicked—and she didn't mind telling me so.

Having gotten her attention, I then let her in on another secret—a secret related to that great little hex-breaker of mine. Simply put, it's this: that nasty-feeling energy that fuels the spell can come from anywhere—even from the magical practitioner casting it. What that means, of course, is that we can even use that slimy crap we douse ourselves with during periods of panic, anxiety, and paranoia. And what could be better than that?!

The Swifting of Energy

If you think you may be the victim of a hex or curse—or if you're having a particularly nasty run of bad luck—then this is the spell for you. But before you perform it, there are a few things you should know. Not to worry. It's nothing awful, and I'm not going to warn you about anything. It's just that it's best to field any possible questions at the onset. That way, there won't be any confusion later.

To start with, this spell may be worked at any time. You don't have to wait for a particular phase of the Moon. You don't have to wait for a specific day of the week. And you certainly don't have to bother with those annoying ceremonial calculations that involve figuring the proper hour, minute, and second. This spell works well no matter when it's performed. And since you're more than likely using it to remove some nasty crap from your life, waiting around for the planets to cooperate simply isn't an option. That's good news.

Another thing is that this spell is absolutely foolproof. There's no way you can screw it up, and you don't have to be a magical genius to get results. All you have to do is follow the directions, know that you're going to get exactly what you asked for, and relax. That's good news too.

Now then . . . I promised that I wouldn't warn you about anything, and I'm as good as my word. However, I do have a few suggestions that, taken under consideration, will make things much easier for you. And since no author worth her salt would dare to omit information that might be of assistance to her readers, I feel obligated to pass these along to you:

- While size usually doesn't matter, it actually does here—but only as far as the candles go. Because they must burn until they extinguish themselves, it's in your best interest to avoid using votive candles. Use small tapers instead. They burn quickly, and you won't have to hang around all day just to make sure that your house doesn't catch fire.

- It's not a good idea to perform this spell for someone else. There's good reason for that. No matter how intimately you're connected to the person you have in mind, there's no way you can truly feel their angst and fury or the full impact of those emotions on their life. And since the power of the spell feeds upon those emotions and the specific way that they affect the person in question, the effects of the spell simply aren't as strong when performed by someone else.

- If you're thinking of working this spell for multiple purposes all at the same time, you may want to reconsider. It's not that it won't work. But in order for it to work as planned, you'll have to be able to visualize every purpose on your list realistically, vividly, and in its entirety from start to finish. That's not only going to take some time but will require switching mental gears on a constant basis until you get through the list. And because of that, it's much easier to perform the swifting for one thing at a time.

With all of that out of the way, let's get started. You'll be amazed at how easy it is, how well it works, and how quickly your life returns to normal!

The Swifting Ritual

Materials:

> *1 black candle*
> *1 brown candle (A yellow, gray, or lavender*
> *   candle may be substituted.)*
> *1 white candle*
> *Table salt*
> *Metal cookie sheet*
> *Paper and pen*
> *A large supply of "negative" energy*

Place the cookie sheet horizontally on a flat surface. Beginning at the center left-hand side of the cookie sheet, arrange the candles—first black, then brown, then white—so they form a horizontal line. Then, using the salt, draw a horizontal line from the white candle to a point approximately three-quarters of the way to the right-hand edge of the pan. Draw an arrow tip with the salt at the end of the line, then draw a salt circle around the arrow tip to encase it.

Write your desire on the paper in large block letters. In all actuality, this can be anything—money, a new job, love, protection, good health, religious tolerance, etc.—as long as it's something for which you have a need. But since we're breaking a curse here, simply write "GOOD FORTUNE." Fold the paper into thirds, then into thirds again, and place it inside the salt circle directly on top of the arrow tip.

Ground and center. Light the black candle and focus on all the nasty energy coming your way. See the harm it's done, the trouble it's caused, and feel your personal misery. Then take it a step further and feel the anger. Don't just become angry though. Let the fury consume you until you're absolutely, positively, livid pissed. Throw a screaming, stomping, hissy fit if that's what it takes to get you there. Then name the candle for negativity.

Light the brown candle. Take a deep breath and exhale slowly, releasing every particle of anger from your body. When detachment takes over—and it will—feel the weight of your personal burdens lighten. Then see the energy begin to transform into something neutral, and name the candle for transformation.

Light the white candle. See the energy transformation process as complete. There is nothing left but clear, bright, raw, pure energy now. Energy that you can use to manifest your desire. Name the candle for raw, untapped, pure energy.

With your eyes, follow the salt line from the candle to the circle, and focus on the paper with your intention. Visualization is very important here, for you not only need to see your desires coming to fruition—your luck changing, your life becoming yours again, living a life you want to live—but also must be able to feel them as if they've already manifested.

Let the candles burn until they extinguish themselves. It's important to note that occasionally one or more will burn out prematurely. But if that should happen, do NOT relight it. Just leave it alone, know it's not a problem, and don't worry about it. It doesn't mean that anything's gone wrong or that the spell isn't working. More than likely, it simply means that an air bubble was trapped during the pouring phase. Neither should you worry if one candle burns out before another. In this case, it has no magical significance.

When the candles extinguish themselves, light the paper, and leave it in the salt circle until it burns to ash. (It's imperative that the paper is completely reduced to ash. If it's not, just light the paper again and allow it to burn until it is.) Once the ashes are cool, gather them together with the salt and the remnants of the wicks and wax (if there are any), and bury the items outdoors. Alternatively, bury the leftovers in a potted plant. (Don't worry about harming the plant, for it's been my experience that once used as this spell's receptacle, even African violets grow more lushly than before.)

Burying the items is, perhaps, the most important part of this spell as it acts to ground the magic. And once it's done, things begin to change immediately. There's no waiting period as is normal for other spells. All that's left is for you to decide precisely how you want to live that life you've taken back. And I've no doubt that you can manage that!

Homeland Security the Witch's Way

Now that you've swifted the energy to put your life back on track, it's probably a good idea to take some precautionary measures to keep it that way. And that means safe-guarding yourself, your home, and your property from the possibility of any future hexes or magical aggravation.

The first thing on the agenda requires a good housecleaning. Please don't groan, and whatever you do, don't try to figure a way around this. I don't like cleaning any better than the next person, but once you've been attacked, it's imperative. Otherwise, you're only going to seal that nasty stuff into your home with any protective measures you take. Even worse, though, anything you do to protect your space is actually going to protect that crap as well. And once that happens, you're going to have a hell of a time getting rid of it. It's best to just buck up, follow the directions, and get this mess over and done with.

Here's something that may make you feel better, though. What's required does not constitute that deep-down-polish-until-it-sparkles Spring cleaning. You won't have to clean closets or cabinets, and you won't have to rearrange your pantry. You won't have to wash curtains, scrub blinds, or polish the furniture. This is just a normal sort of housecleaning with a few twists. And since you don't have to do all that other stuff, it won't take but an hour or two. Just use the checklist below and you'll be done before you know it.

Open the windows. While fresh air is a good thing and always makes the house smell better, this has nothing to do with that. Instead, it's a matter of providing an escape route for all that negative stuff living within its boundaries. The idea here is to force any unsavory energy to leave, and if you don't provide a means by which it can do that, you've only served to keep it trapped inside with you. So even if it's cold outside, raise the windows at least an inch.

Light a vanilla candle. There's little that negative energy likes less than the scent of vanilla, so this will give it the impetus to leave.

Clear the air. To chase out unsavory energy, burn Fiery Wall of Protection Incense (see recipe in Chapter 5) on a charcoal block as you work. Place the censer or fireproof dish on a heat-proof trivet in the middle of your home, and keep the incense going until you've finished cleaning.

Remove the clutter. This is important since negative energy thrives in this sort of mess. For the moment, though, don't bother to go through it all. (If you do, you'll never get done.) Just toss it in a box for now and get it out of the way. You can go through it after you've completed the rest of the list.

Powder the carpets. Sprinkle Peaceful Home Powder (see recipe in Chapter 5) on carpets and rugs, then vacuum thoroughly.

Get rid of the dust and sweep the floors. Negative energy thrives in grit and grime too, and refusing to take care of this will only exacerbate your problem.

Mop the floors. Along with your cleaning solution, add one cup of your urine and a teaspoon of hot sauce to a gallon of water, and use the mixture to handle the job. While this may sound a little odd, the reasons are sound. Urine is not only natural ammonia, but using your own also saturates the living quarters with your personal power and safeguards your home from anything you don't invite. But adding the hot sauce takes the protection process a step further. Because it acts like Hot Foot Powder, it handles unwanted guests by forcing them to leave. (Note: The combination of urine and hot sauce tends to leave a powdery residue. So once completely dry, sweep the floors again.)

Wipe down fixtures and countertops. Nothing odd about this at all. Just use your favorite cleaning solution.

Clean the drains. For this task, you'll need lemons. To determine how many, just count the drains in your home—be sure to include the toilets and the dishwasher—and divide by two. Cut each lemon in half, squeeze the juice of one portion down each drain, and flush well with hot water. This will take care of any nasties living in your pipes.

Tend to your hairbrushes. Remove the hair and burn it, then clean your brushes with hot, soapy water and bleach. While this may sound strange, it actually handles several potential problems. First, the hairbrush is one of the places that nasty energy likes to live, so you'll be uprooting it from one of its favorite hiding places. Second, burning the hair removes its connection to you. But third and just as important, getting rid of the hair also removes other possible connections to you. It prevents a visitor using the bathroom as a guise, grabbing some of the hair from your brush, and using it against you. And while you may think that sounds like paranoia at work, I assure you that's not the case. It happens a lot more often than folks think, and there's simply no point in taking that chance.

Clean the walls. Okay . . . at this point, I can almost see the wheels turning in your head as you try to figure a way around this. Not to worry though. You won't have to scrub. Just mix a handful of table salt into a spray bottle filled with hot water. Then give it a good shake and spritz the walls. Done deal.

Take out the trash. This removes any leftover residue that might still be hanging around.

Shield with bay leaves. Place one leaf in each corner of every room in your home to protect from hexes, curses, and other magical annoyances. As an additional perk, bay leaf also draws money.

Safeguard your doors. After all this cleaning, the last thing you want is for any more crap to cross your thresholds. And because harmful energy shouldn't cross either, you'll need to prepare a 50:50 mixture of red brick dust and table salt. (Since you're only going to sprinkle a little of the substance under each of your outside doormats, you won't need a lot; in fact, a cup of the mixture ought to be more than enough to do the trick.) If you don't have red bricks at your disposal, obtain one from your local building supply. Then put it in a heavy paper bag, and pulverize it using a hammer.

Safeguard your property. If you live in a house, sprinkle salt around the outside perimeter of the property. If an apartment, townhouse, or condo is more your style, sprinkle the salt around your baseboards or inside wall edges instead.

So, you've cleaned your home. You've gotten rid of every last shred of that bothersome energy. All that's left to do is close the windows, sit back, relax, and enjoy that wonderful new feeling coursing through your home. Right?

Not exactly.

Remember that box of clutter? While some of you will undoubtedly leave that for another time, I urge you to tend to it now. It won't take but a few minutes to toss out what you don't need and put the rest away. If you don't, you'll only be providing a breeding ground for additional problems. And after all the trouble you just went to, I seriously doubt that you'll want to do that!

Wash That Crap Right
Out of Your Life

Now that you've got a clean house, it's time for a nice hot bath. Already showered? That's not a problem. Just as with the rest of the psychic baths mentioned in this book, you'll need to be clean before you step into the tub. Unlike the others, however, this one is meant to be long and luxurious. And even though its purpose is to cleanse you of any psychic crap that may still be clinging to you and crossing you up, it's meant to be enjoyed. Before you're done, in fact, you may even find yourself reaching up with your toe to turn on the hot water again.

While you won't have any problem obtaining most of the items on the materials list, finding blue balls may be somewhat of a hassle if you don't know what you're looking for. To compound the problem, metaphysical and occult retailers occasionally sell these little goodies under other names. So, to avoid confusion, it's probably a good idea to explain exactly what they are. Blue balls are nothing more than small, round, button-like balls made from compressed, powdered bluing. (It's the same stuff that folks used to put in the final rinse to whiten and brighten white laundry.) And if, by chance, your local retailer doesn't carry them? Liquid bluing can still be purchased online.

The Blue Uncrossing Bath

Materials:

> 2 blue balls (or 1 teaspoon liquid bluing)
> 1 teaspoon jasmine petals (or 2 drops jasmine oil)
> 1 teaspoon lemon peel
> 1 teaspoon rose petals
> 1 tablespoon salt
> 1 teaspoon thyme
> Vanilla candles (optional)
> Bubble bath (optional)

Place the first six ingredients in the filter cup of the automatic drip coffeemaker, and add a full pot of water. When the brew cycle is finished, add the contents of the pot to a hot tub of water, and mix well. If you've opted for bubble bath and candles, put them to use now as well.

Completely immerse yourself at least three times in the water, then sit back, relax, and say the following prayer:

> *Oh, Virgin Goddess, Maiden pure,*
> *Look down on me and lend your cure*
> *To heal my life, to heal my soul,*
> *To heal my body from the toll*
> *That wretched magic's wreaked on them,*
> *Wash them clean like sparkling gems.*

Eradicate now every trace
Of psychic filth and quickly chase
All remnants of this nastiness
Far from me where it can't press
Against or block me any more,
Uncross my life and lock the door
On future problems of this kind,
Bar and keep them well confined.
Oh, Virgin, keep me close to You,
Protect me in the things I do.
And with Your blessings shower me,
As I will, so mote it be.

Soak, relax, enjoy your bath. Towel dry when finished.

Security in a Bottle

It's often hard to know who our enemies are, or if we even have any. But the fact of the matter is that even the most wonderful folks in the world have a few. It's not that they did anything to hurt anybody. It's just that jealousy and misconception seem to run rampant within the human race, so we never know who might be annoyed at our successes or who might delight at the thought of our personal demises.

Fortunately, there's an easy way to avoid any possible aggravation and stop enemies in their tracks. And all it takes is making the Witch's Bottle described below. If you've opted to bury it on your property though, take note: you'll want to prepare another if you sell the property or decide to move away.

The Witch's Bottle

Materials:

> *Small glass jar with a tight-fitting, screw-on lid*
> *An assortment of sharp objects (Broken glass and pottery*
> *shards, razor blades, rusty nails and screws, pins and*
> *needles, and wood splinters are all good choices.)*
> *Personal taglocks (A snippet of your hair and/or*
> *your fingernail clippings will do nicely.)*
> *Your urine*
> *Optional for women only: a tissue containing a*
> *few drops of your menstrual blood*
> *Optional for men only: a tissue containing*
> *a few drops of your semen*
> *Duct or electrical tape, or melted wax*

Fill the jar at least half full of the sharp objects, place the taglocks on top, and if you wish, add the blood or semen. Finish filling the jar with your urine, and screw the jar lid on tightly. Then seal the lid well with tape or wax.

Since it's important that the container remain intact, tradition holds that it should be buried at least a foot deep on your property and as close to the front door as possible. If you live in an apartment, though, what's traditional may not be at all feasible. In that case, simply put the jar out of the way—the back of a cabinet or closet, or on a dark shelf works well—and leave it there to do its thing.

Fixing the Mother of All Screwups

No matter how well we research our facts nor how careful we try to be, we're eventually going to screw up. It's just a part of the human condition. And there's no place our screwups shine more brightly than in the hexes and curses arena.

That's because standing up for ourselves doesn't always come easily. Most of us really do take an awful lot of crap before finally deciding to do something about it. And even then, we don't get in a hurry. We go about our business, gathering the facts and exploring our options. We peruse the details with the same sort of attention we might exhaust on a multimillion-dollar business venture. And then, when we're sure that everything's in order, we start the magical process, feeling absolutely safe in the fact that we're completely justified in our actions and that our target (damn his rotten bananas!) deserves every shred we're doling out, and then some. If we weren't and he didn't, things would never have gotten to this point. So, we do our thing and go on along our merry ways, never giving it a second thought.

But then one day, it happens. An ugly head breaks through the muck, stares us right in the face, and blinks. And we—those same folks who felt completely justified in damning that target's rotten bananas—can barely catch our collective breath as we gasp in horror. For there, right in the eyes of the beast, we see our mistake: the target was undeniably innocent. He was never even involved in the fiasco that damned near ruined our lives. Instead, he was just another innocent bystander; just some good, old Joe who was in the wrong place at the right time. A good, old Joe who we forced to pay for someone else's infractions with a close encounter of the very worst kind. And there we sit, shivering and shaking and wracking our brains, in a desperate search of some way to fix things, wondering how in the hell we could've been so wrong.

To start with, today's world is an interesting place. With its high-flung technology and far-flung virtual realities, some might even say that it's nothing short of amazing. But living in such a world also has complications, the most problematical being that, because things are seldom as they appear, it becomes increasingly difficult to separate fact from fiction. Now take that problem and factor in a fact-finding mission, a little logic, and a few rounds of he-said-she-said, and add them all together. I can nearly guarantee that the sum of those components isn't going to be at all within the scope of reason. Reasonable or not, though, it appears to be the truth. And because it appears as such, we act on it as such—only to discover later that it was the most wretched mistake we ever made.

While that takes care of how easy it is to screw up—and hopefully, has illustrated just how important it is to factor in gut instinct as well as the facts—we still have a problem on our hands: How in the hell do we fix the mess we made? More to the point, though, is it even possible?

Fortunately, it is. Please understand, though, that it won't be easy, regardless of how simple the instructions appear. There's absolutely no way to convey the degree of difficulty involved in rectifying something like this. So, just be prepared to work long and hard, and as some effects can never be truly erased, be willing to repeat some steps you've already taken over and over to ease the problem if the need arises.

The Poppet and Packet Racket

If the magic you worked involved the use of a poppet or a packet (a mojo or gris gris bag, or a collection of objects), feel fortunate. The good news is that it's one of the easier types of magic to unravel. But don't breathe that sigh of relief just yet. The bad news is that you're going to have to retrieve the objects and destroy them. And if you buried them—or even worse, already destroyed them—that could present a problem.

But just for grins, let's say that you haven't destroyed the objects, you know exactly where they are, and you can put your hands on them. In this case, breaking the magic is only a matter of destroying the objects. You'll only have one shot at this, though, so you'll need to do it correctly.

Destroying a Packet: While there are many techniques, I believe that the most thorough way to break the magic is to completely dismantle the packet. Start by removing the contents piece by piece. Set each piece on fire and allow it to burn to ash, then continue with any other pieces one at a time. When nothing else remains, burn the bag or packet covering if there is one. Finally, toss the ashes into running water to disperse them.

Destroying a Poppet or Doll: Remember how you marked the object with the target's name? Well, the first order of business is to get rid of that. So, mark through it with a heavy, black permanent marker, and continue to work until none of the identifying name shows through. Once that's done, remove any identifying marks if possible. Finally, burn the doll to ash and toss the remains in running water.

Putting a Hex or a Curse
in Magical Reverse

If you've resorted to this section, you obviously can't retrieve the remnants of your original spell. You may have delivered a curse on the power of words alone. You may have opted to go the gift route and delivered something with a built-in hex. In either case, though, you have absolutely nothing to work with that's going to be of any help. This means that you're going to need a lot of resolve, some serious focus, and the tenacity of the most willful bulldog. But if you're willing to work at this, there's no doubt you'll succeed.

The first thing you'll need to have in hand is a copy of any words (incantations, evocations, verbal curses, etc.) that you may have said while casting the original spell. If you kept a copy of it, grab it now, and thank the Gods for making you so anal-retentive. If you didn't, though, do your best to call it up, and spend some time writing it down.

Next, obtain an old, knitted sweater. The color isn't important. Neither is the size. In this case, only two things matter: 1) you have never actually worn the sweater, and 2) you're willing to reduce it to yarn. If you don't already have something suitable on hand, check your local thrift shop.

Once you have the sweater, gather the paper on which the incantations are written and a black permanent marker. Now write the words on the sweater. It's not important that they're legible; it's only important that they've been written on the sweater and that you have done it yourself. Use the front and back if necessary.

When you've finished, perform the ritual below. Know that this may take some time—depending upon the size of the sweater, it may take several hours—so be sure to allow enough to do the job well.

Curse Unraveling Ritual

Materials:

> *1 black/white reversible candle (If you can't find one of*
> *these, substitute a white candle which you've colored*
> *completely with a black permanent marker.)*
> *1 yellow candle*
> *Uncrossing Incense*
> *Charcoal block*
> *Fireproof dish*
> *Cauldron or firepit*
> *Scissors*
> *Sweater*

Light the reversible candle and visualize the magic reversing itself. Light the yellow candle and see the effort meeting with success. Then light the charcoal block and sprinkle the incense on top.

Now sit in a comfortable position in front of the cauldron or firepit. Using the scissors, cut the neck and cuff ribbing away from the sweater and toss them into the receptacle. Locate a yarn end on the garment and begin to unravel the fabric, saying something like:

> *The magic cast now falls away*
> *As I unravel it today,*
> (name of target)*'s life is now returned*

As magic in the cauldron's burned.
By all the power of Moon and Sun
I remove all harm; so be it done.

Continue to repeat the chant as you unravel the sweater, stopping occasionally to snip off the loosened yarn and set it aflame in the cauldron. Continue the process until the sweater is completely unraveled, burned, and reduced to ash. Either discard the ashes in running water or scatter them on the winds.

Part Two

When footsteps come

Within the night

And you're beset

By doubt and fright

Just hold fast within

That hour

For to the Witch

All fear is POWER

David O. Norris © 1998

Chapter 7

The Bad, the Nasty, and the Downright Ugly

Before We Begin . . .

While I've used the terms "hex" and "curse" interchangeably throughout this book, I've done so as a matter of convenience. But it's important to note that most practitioners don't use them in that fashion. They view the terms as two entirely separate entities with completely different meanings. And I'd be remiss in my duties as an author if I failed to share this information.

For most practitioners, a curse relies solely upon the spoken word or, in the case of the Evil Eye, a personal gesture. They say that nothing else is necessary when cursing someone, as the emotion behind the words or act is the force that drives it. Of course, this means that the curse must be delivered with a heaping helping of anger or hatred to hit its mark—and even more to have true staying power.

According to this same contingent, a hex is the product of a spell or ritual. And while it is certainly directed and powered by the emotional state of the practitioner, it also makes use of additional aids such as personal effects, powders, washes, charms, and so forth. Of course, putting a ritual together takes a lot more time than simply letting a few words fly from the tongue. But even so, having this extra help is often well worth the effort for a couple of reasons: First, it allows for a cooling off period and time to think things through before actually putting the magic in motion. Second, there's no need to shoulder the whole burden of driving the magic to its mark since the properties of other ingredients assist with that. And third, it completely eliminates the need to come to a screeching halt right in the middle of a good hissy fit, just in order to curse the target. All things considered, it's no wonder that hexes have become the more popular form of magic for these particular practitioners.

But here's where things get dicey. There's another magical sector that subscribes to the "hexes for good or bad" theory. It's their belief that a hex is nothing more than a symbol and, as in the case of Pennsylvania Dutch hex signs, can be used to deliver magic on both ends of the spectrum. A curse, they say, is any magic powered by the fuel of ill intent.

There's also a sector who believes that if the desired result even borders upon the unsavory, a related Bible verse must be incorporated into the effort to achieve effectiveness. Another sector believes that specific deities must be called upon to get results. And so on. And so on. And so on.

Trying to figure out who's right and who's wrong is enough to make your head spin. After months of research, though, I did finally come to a conclusion: No matter how you slice it or dress it for the altar, it's still all a matter of semantics. Everybody's right. Nobody's wrong. So when it comes to choosing a school of thought, just pick whichever most closely resembles your own way of thinking, and know that you'll do just fine.

No matter how many schools of thought there are nor how diverse the thinking, there is, however, one common thread that runs through all. Simply put, it's this: Focus is key when it comes to working magic. And nothing—not taglocks, nor potions, nor the Deities, Themselves—is going to make your magic work if you can't manage it successfully. So if you're having trouble with this, I urge you to work with the exercises listed at the end of Chapter 4 before going any further. Otherwise, the magical collection that follows isn't going to do you one damned bit of good. It's only going to serve to waste your time and energy—and no one I know has enough of either to waste.

One Other Thing

I don't perform hexes and curses for other people. And you shouldn't either.

Yes, I know that sounds self-righteous. But to be perfectly honest, I don't care. I'd much rather weather that accusation than be forced to deal with the possibility of my words being twisted. I'd much rather weather that than be faced with the possibility of a misunderstanding. Or even worse, the possibility of having failed you. To that end, let me make this perfectly clear:

Do NOT, under any circumstances, perform a hex or curse for someone else!

Some of the reasons are obvious, and we've already touched on them. First, no one is truly capable of feeling the depth of someone else's angst, and that level of feeling is absolutely necessary for complete and total success. Second, forming a connection to somebody else's crap is not a place you want to go. It doesn't matter how much you care for them or how much you want to see them relieved of their current dilemma. Doing so is not only tantamount to taking their place in the magical arena—and absorbing more residue than you can ever get rid of—but also making their decisions for them. And you simply don't have the right to do that. No one does.

But if that's not enough to stop you, then try this on for size: nobody likes a busybody!

Okay, I'll admit it. That was a little harsh. But since no truer statement has ever been spoken or been more applicable to the subject matter at hand, it had to be said.

The truth is that we, as members of the human race, are do-gooders at heart, and there's nothing wrong with that. We worry about the fact that our brother is screwing over his partner and refuses to see the problem. We worry about our daughter, who's in an abusive marriage and can't seem to summon the courage to leave. We worry about our best friend, who's being taken advantage of financially. And on and on and on. Our worries are completely justified; in fact, there would be something drastically wrong with us if we weren't at all concerned.

However, these sorts of concerns have no personal place in the magical arena. More to the point, though, they have no personal place in the spiritual arena. And when we take things to the magical level for someone else—when we take it upon ourselves to butt into his or her business—it's the spiritual realm with which we get into trouble.

You see, just as each person on this Earth is a complete and separate individual, the same is true of the lives they've been offered. No two people share precisely the same sort of life or the same life lessons. They don't have the same paths to choose from and don't meet the same trials and tribulations along the way. Each is set up on an individual basis, specifically designed with one person in mind. And because of that, each person is also given a particular set of talents and strengths to draw upon in living that life and learning its lessons.

This means that there's not a single person on this Earth who's been dealt a hand they cannot play. It's just a matter of deciding which card to play and when. Of course, the cards in our hands aren't always winners. Sometimes we don't even have good choices. Still and all, though, we have to play what we've been dealt whether we want to or not, and do so to the best of our ability. Otherwise, we can't learn our lessons, and the life we've been given becomes a farce.

That brings me back to the busybody remark. If we take things to the magical level for someone else, we are, in essence, taking control of their lives. We are playing their hands for them and, in all probability, keeping them from learning their life lessons. It doesn't matter that we're doing it for all the right reasons. What does matter is that we're way out of line and doing those we love a great injustice.

So when it comes to hexes and curses, do everyone near and dear to you a favor: keep your nose out of their business, and plant it squarely in your own life. If you don't, know that while you'll definitely pay a price for your indiscretion, they're the ones who will pay the most. And it will cost them much more than you ever dreamed possible.

Finally

What you'll find on the following pages is a collection of curses, hexes, magical manipulations, and related information. And while each and every spell included works beautifully as written, nothing works as well as the magical effort you've designed specifically for yourself. For that reason, don't be afraid to expand upon these and restructure them to suit your own purpose and lifestyle. Know that your own version will not only work, but is likely to be even more personally effective than the version printed here.

Ready? Set? Let's get started!

Automobiles, Parking Lots, and Traffic

Lady Dame's Freeway Curse

Lights of red and blue that fly:
Come through here and pass me by,
Catch the one who rides the wind
Pull their ass over and ticket them!

Lady Dame's Parking Space Curse

The space you stole—
Not yours alone—
A scratch, you'll find,
Down to the bone!

Automobile Curse

While this curse may give you the giggles, don't discount its effectiveness. It's perfect for the guy who seems to love his vehicle more than you!

I curse your wheels! I curse your car
With dings and dents and scratches that mar.
That pretty paint job that you love,
I curse it around, between, below, above.
With tires that will not hold their air,
With thin upholstery that will tear,
With gauges that don't measure right,
Or tell you if your fuel is light,
Or tell you if your speed is high.
And oil that leaks 'til you could cry,
With gaskets that won't hold a seal,
With wiper blades that bend and peel,
With a defrost button that won't defog.
A horn that sounds just like a frog,
Heat and air that never work.
And if that's not enough, you jerk:
I curse you with a trade-in deal
So bad you'll think that it's not real,
And you'll be stuck right where you are
Alone with her—that lovely car!

Bad Habits

Toilet Paper Hex

Materials:

> *Length of toilet paper*
> *Pen*

Write a full description of the bad habit on the toilet paper, then use it to wipe yourself. Flush it down the toilet.

Spend No More Hex

Use this spell on a partner who's spending you right into the poor house.

Materials:

> *Poppet*
> *Hot sauce*
> *Green permanent marker*
> *Black permanent marker*
> *Small paintbrush*
> *Black cloth*

Prepare the poppet in the target's likeness, then using the black marker, draw a pocket on each side of the front hip (the point where pants pockets are located) and on each buttock. Using the green marker, draw a dollar sign in the center of each pocket, on the forehead, and in the palm of each hand. Pick up the black marker again, and forcefully draw a large black X through each of the dollar signs, and say with each:

No more money shall you spend.
Your fun and games are at an end.
No more credit! No more cash!
No more money shall you stash!

Now sprinkle the paintbrush with a few drops of hot sauce, and paint over the pockets and the crossed-out dollar signs. (Give the symbols on the head and hands an extra coat for good measure.) As you paint, say:

If you even think to spend,
Your comfort zones are at an end:
Your head shall ache without relief,
Your hands shall itch and bring you grief,
The pockets on your thighs shall burn;
And if that's not enough concern,
The heat will travel and conspire
To make you think your ass caught fire!
Don't even think to spend a dime
For no reprieve will come this time.
The symptoms shall just be increased
And for you, there is no release!

Wrap the poppet in a black cloth and hide on the property.

Business Dealings Gone Bad

Mary Caliendo's Runic Business Hex

This is a wonderful tool to use when you've been screwed in business. The best part is that the runes, themselves, do most of the work for you!

Materials:

> *Copy of the contract in question, signed by the target*
> *Copy of the target's business card*
> *Paper*
> *Red permanent marker*
> *Cauldron or fireproof dish*

Hold the contract in your hands, look at the signature, and see it for what it is: a form of the target's energy that's being used to invoke Karma by his or her own hand. Red marker in hand and using the illustration below as a guideline, draw the Pertho rune (symbolizing that which is hidden), the Dag rune (symbolizing that which turns around), and the Solowuz rune (symbolizing that which is illuminated or brings the light of day) across the contract at a downward slant, beginning at the upper left-hand corner and ending at the lower right-hand corner. (This will shed light on any shady dealings, bring them to the forefront, and expose all involved.)

Spit on the runes to "feed" them, then burn the contract in the cauldron while chanting:

All that is hidden shall come to the light,
All that is hidden shall come to the light,
All that is hidden shall come to the light.
Their Action exposed,
Their injustice exposed,
Their deceit is exposed.

Now draw the Isa rune (see illustration below) in the center of the business card. (As Isa means "ice," this rune brings the target to a screeching halt and freezes his or her every action. The target is now unable to hide anything further or deceive anyone—and unable to harm others.)

Spit on the rune, set the business card on fire, and throw it in the cauldron. As it burns, chant:

Your character is seen clear as ice,
Not backwards or forwards are you able to move,
Until you make amends for all that you do.
Your shady dealings, to the ground, all fell,
The authorities will surely know as well.

Draw the Hagalaz rune (see illustration below) on the paper. (As this rune represents hail, it causes complete and total chaos.)

ᚼ

Spit on the rune, light the paper, and toss it into the cauldron as well. As it burns, beseech Dame Holda, the Nordic Goddess Who causes hail with a shake of Her bed, to help you. Say:

Dame Holda, as You shake Your bed,
Rain Your hail upon their heads,
But only if it is observed
That this is justice and should be served.

Finally, call on the Norns (sometimes known as the Wyrd Sisters), Who feed, spin, and cut the threads of our existence—the threads which we, ourselves, offer Them—to intercede as well by saying:

Norns of three, s/he's woven his/her fate
By his/her own hands s/he did create,
Invoke his/her wyrd, then cut the thread
So others shan't be harmed or misled.

When the ashes are cool, flush them down the toilet, and know the problem will be handled.

Chaos, Mayhem, and General Confusion

Knots of Chaos

This is a fabulous spell to use on someone who has hurt others for his or her own benefit.

Materials:

   Length of jute or hemp cord cut to the height of your target

Find the center of the cord and tie the first knot there, saying:

   By knot of one, you come undone,

Tie the second knot to the right of the first, saying:

   By knot of two, chaos brews,

Tie the third knot to the left of the first, saying:

   By knot of three, you'll want to flee,

Tie the fourth knot to the right of the second, saying:

   But knot of four just locks the door.

Now, alternating to the left and right, tie the remaining knots as follows while chanting the related verse. The fifth knot:

   By knot of five, you lose your drive,

The sixth knot:

   By knot of six, your mind plays tricks,

The seventh knot:

   By knot of seven, you'll wish for heaven,

The eighth knot:

But knot of eight just slams that gate,

The ninth knot:

By knot of nine, your strength declines,

The tenth knot:

By knot of ten, you cannot win,

The eleventh knot:

By knot of eleven, you'll wish for seven,

The twelfth knot:

But that is shelved by knot of twelve.

The thirteenth knot:

It's the thirteenth knot that does you in
And leaves you paying for your sins.
It brings you right down to your knees
And leaves you begging for release.
But none shall come until you've paid
For what you've done, the games you've played,
The folks you've hurt, the lives you've frayed.
And only then shall you receive
Your life again and a reprieve.

Dig a hole at least nine inches deep and bury the cord in the ground.

Foot Track Hex

This simple hex torments your enemy by preventing advancement in any sector of his or her life.

Materials:

> *4 coffin nails*
> *Target's foot track*
> *Hammer*

Go to a place where the target has walked, and locate one of his or her foot tracks. Hammer a nail in the top of the track, saying:

> *You can't move up,*

Hammer a nail in the bottom of the track and say:

> *You can't move down,*

Hammer a nail on the right side of the track and say:

> *Nor right,*

Hammer a nail on the left side of the track and say:

> *Nor left,*

Then, moving your hand in a circular motion first to the right and then to the left, say:

> *Nor all around.*
> *You're stuck in place and there you'll be*
> *Forever: For eternity!*

Walk away and don't look back.

Fight Like Cats and Dogs Hex

This hex requires a field trip to a dog park, but the results are well worth the effort!

Materials:

> *Dirt from a dog park*
> *Cat hair (If you don't have a cat, obtain*
> *   this from a friend who does.)*
> *Black pepper*
> *Cayenne or habanero pepper*
> *Salt*
> *Coffee grinder*

Go to a dog park and wait for a dogfight. (Trust me on this: if you stay there long enough, you will surely witness one!) Once the fight is over and the dogs have been led away, collect some dirt from the location of the altercation.

Put the dirt in the coffee grinder along with the hair, salt, and peppers, set the grinder to "fine," and run it for 15 to 30 seconds. While it's running, say:

> *Fuss and argue, hiss and bite,*
> *Bark and snarl and yell and fight!*

Sprinkle the powder anywhere you want to sow dissension and discord. (Be sure to clean your work area thoroughly, so as not to cause the problem in your own home!)

Temporary Blue Jay Feather Hex

Materials:

> *1 blue jay feather*
> *Pen and paper*

Write the target's name, then spear it with the feather, making certain that the paper is securely attached. Hold the feather in both hands and say:

> *No rest for you, no peace in view,*
> *Confusion lives and breathes in you.*
> *Voices in your head erupt*
> *To override and interrupt*
> *Those voices speaking in the now*
> *Distortion rules and won't allow*
> *Common sense to take its place,*
> *And you begin to come unlaced,*
> *Certain that you've lost your mind*
> *And no relief at all, you'll find*
> *Until this paper comes unwound*
> *From feathered stem and falls to ground.*

Plant the feather stem in the ground on the target's property.

Tower Card Hex

To create chaos and mayhem for your target, write his or her name in black ink across a copy of the Tower card of the Tarot, then burn it, and scatter the ashes.

Crow Feather Discord Hex

To sow general discord in the target's home, hide a crow feather in his or her house or slip it under the front porch. To create chaos for the target at work, hide the feather in the appropriate work space. (Note: it's important that the feather be found rather than taken by force; otherwise, the magic could backfire on you.)

Coffin Nails

While coffin nails used to be plentiful and easy to come by, such is not the case anymore. Of course, there are still many occult supply stores that offer them for sale, but the problem with obtaining those is clear: there's no way to know whether the nails you've bought are truly the real thing or just regular nails that can be purchased at half the cost from any local hardware store. This problem can be avoided, however, if you simply make your own. And all it takes is a package of nails, some graveyard dirt, a zippered plastic bag, and the instructions below.

- Count out the number of nails you'll need for the spell in question, and charge them with your desire.

- Place the nails in the plastic bag, and sprinkle them well with graveyard dirt appropriate to your desire. (A few tablespoons will do it.)

- If the spell calls for rusty nails, sprinkle well with water.

- Seal the bag, allow the nails to rest in the dirt overnight, and they'll be ready for use the next day. (Note: do not wipe the nails clean before use.)

While we're on the subject of nails, you should probably know that those gathered from particular sites can definitely add power to your magic. For your convenience, a few collection sites along with their uses follow below:

Courthouse: To bring justice or to cause the target to lose his or her legal battle.

Hospital: To cause illness.

Jail: To bring jail or prison time.

Mental institution: To cause insanity.

Police station: To bring about an arrest.

Workplace: To cause trouble for a coworker or employer.

Court Cases and the Legal System

Red Brick Victory Spell

Materials:

> *1 yellow candle*
> *2 red bricks*
> *Commanding/Controlling/Compelling Powder*
> *Pen and paper*

Make a list of everyone on the opposing legal team. Include attorneys, witnesses, and the person who opposes you. Then cross the names out one by one, spit on each, and say:

> *I cross you and I cover you*
> *So that your tongue is still*

And cannot speak against me
No matter your true will.

Sprinkle the list liberally with the powder, then fold it in half twice. Dust one of the bricks with the powder, place the paper on top, then sprinkle the paper again. Place the second brick on top, saying:

With these bricks I block and bar
All evidence against me,
So the only facts admissible
Are those that would relieve me
Of the charges on the books
And guarantee my victory.

Place the yellow candle directly on top of the bricks and light the wick, saying:

Wax melt quickly—seal the spell—
Scorch the tongues of those who'd tell
Anything not boding well,
Anything that might repel
A legal victory for me,
Melt quickly all adversity
To my success immediately
So a favorable ruling there will be
And mine shall be the victory.

Allow the candle to extinguish itself, and place the brick parcel by your front door.

Opposing Attorney Hex

Materials:

1 black candle
Crossing Oil
Graveyard dirt
Copy of a legal document signed by opposing attorney

Anoint the candle with Crossing Oil and light the wick. Rub a little bit of the oil across the attorney's signature, then dip your finger into the dirt, and smear that across the signature as well. Say:

Someone has to win this case
And someone has to lose,
So wipe that glib look off your face
For you shall sing the blues:
You're unprepared, you cannot speak
With eloquence, your case is weak.
In the court, you look a fool
With all objections overruled.
You hem and haw, you stutter much,
You worry that you've lost your touch.
Your confidence is at a low
(How could it be you're eating crow?)
Nothing works the way it should,
Your witnesses aren't any good.
The judge eyes you with aggravation
Until at last, with resignation
You admit your own defeat
And give to me the victory, sweet.

Leave the document in front of the candle until the wick burns out, then bury it as close to the courthouse as possible. If that's not an option, bury it at a crossroads in the cemetery.

Tongue-Loosening Witness Hex

This is an excellent spell for enticing a reluctant witness to testify for you in court.

Materials:

> *1 box chocolate-coated laxative*
> *Pen and paper*
> *Plastic zippered bag*
> *Small plastic or glass bowl*

Unwrap all of the laxative, place the pieces in the zippered bag, and set the bag in the bowl. (Do not zip the bag!) Heat the laxative in the microwave for a few seconds at a time until it's completely melted.

Write the name of the reluctant witness on the paper, and slip it inside the bag. Press the air out of the bag, zip it shut, and squish the contents until the name is completely coated, saying:

> *Your tongue is loosened, you shall speak*
> *The testimony that I seek,*
> *Quickly, freely, without qualm*
> *Otherwise, your bowels so calm,*
> *Shall churn and cramp and lose control—*
> *A constant, messy rigmarole—*
> *Until diarrhea of the mouth*
> *Ends your problems of the south.*

Place the bag with any legal documents pertaining to the case.

Southern John Spell

To have a judge rule in your favor, arrive at the courtroom early, and spend the time chewing a piece of Southern John root (also known as Little John). As you chew, see yourself as the victor. Spit it out onto the floor before the judge enters the room.

Criminals

Serial Rapist Go to Hell Spell
(Based on a spell from the collection of Mary Caliendo)

Even though this spell was created to stop a serial rapist, it can easily be tweaked to stop serial killers and other extreme evil-doers as well.

Materials:

> *Fabric poppet (readily available at most occult stores)*
> *Newspaper sketch of the criminal's face*
> *Black yarn*
> *Black thread*
> *Black permanent marker*
> *Needle*
> *Hot glue*
> *1 teaspoon graveyard dirt*
> *Potting soil*
> *Aluminum foil*
> *Jar with tight-fitting screw-on lid*

Cut out the newspaper sketch of the criminal's face, then scan and reduce it to fit the face area of the poppet. Cut out the face and hot glue it in position. Make a slit in the back of the poppet, add the graveyard dirt, then stitch up the hole with black thread. Bind the hands and feet with black yarn, and tie tightly to secure. Now using the black marker and the illustration below, draw the Eihwaz (death) rune on the genital area.

$$\int$$

Then say:

> Three blows you've dealt unto the world
> So your true colors come unfurled:
> Your mind is evil, your heart is black,
> Your actions, despicable—and with all that,
> You've bought your own reward today
> And delivery shall come without delay:
> Plucked from our world like a flea from a dog,
> Sucked from our presence like a stick in the bog,
> Imprisoned by bars, imprisoned in fear—
> Where screams are unheard by those far and those near,
> Where no one's concerned if you live or you die,
> And you're not worth the effort to spit in your eye—
> And there you shall sit in your personal hell,
> In more pain and misery than mere words can tell,
> Imprisoned forever without hope of release
> A fitting reward for a monstrous beast!

Line both the inside of the jar and the lid with foil, shiny side facing in. Fill the jar half full of potting soil, toss the poppet in, then finish filling the jar. Light the black candle, and use it to drip wax around the inside of the lid, then screw the lid tightly onto the jar. Blow out the candle and set the jar by your door.

Cheating Gambler Curse

You're probably wondering what on Earth this hex is doing in the *Criminals* section. It's no mistake, and I really haven't lost my mind. It's just that I have no use for folks who cheat at cards and games of chance, and I believe they are criminals of the worst kind, who do, in fact, belong behind bars. But since the law won't put them there, I'm doing my part by putting them here!

No materials are necessary for effectiveness. Just visualize the target up to his or her antics, and curse him or her firmly and forcefully by saying:

A liar, cheat, and common thief
Is what you are; You deal out grief,
You only play to steal the pot.
And with this curse, you shall be caught.
I curse you to the nth degree
And your cards shall fall accordingly:
No more Aces, no more pairs,
No more flushes—not a prayer—
No more help for a boat or a straight,
Only poor hands are now your fate.
And if you dare again to cheat,

All will see you from their seat
At the table and raise hell.
Alarms will sound and all will tell
Others of what scum you are;
All will know from near and far,
And refuse to share a game with you.
And with the cards, you shall be through!

Debt Retrieval

Birdseed Hex

Materials:

> *Prepared poppet, unclothed*
> *1 cup peanut butter*
> *1½ cups birdseed*
> *¼ yard fabric netting (Note: do not use tulle!)*
> *Length of black ribbon*
> *Glass or plastic mixing bowl*
> *Old newspapers*

As this is a messy sort of project, begin by covering your work area with old newspapers. Place the peanut butter in the bowl, then put it in the microwave for five to ten seconds to soften. Add one cup of the birdseed, and mix well while chanting:

> *A treat for you, my feathered friends,*
> *I mix today so hunger ends*
> *And so you'll come from near and far*
> *And help me wage this personal war!*

Working on the newspapers, apply the mixture to the poppet, covering it completely and paying special attention to the hair, face, and feet. Continue the process until the mixture is completely gone. (By the time you're finished, the shape of the poppet should no longer be recognizable.) Say:

Food for the birds, you now become
To be picked at until I've won.
No rest, no peace—it starts today—
Just constant picking 'til you pay
Every dollar you owe to me,
Only then, shall you be free.

Roll the poppet in the rest of the birdseed, then place it in the center of the net. Draw up the edges, and tie them securely with the ribbon, saying:

I catch you up and jail you tight,
There's no escape now from this rite.
You'll swing freely from the tree—
A bird's delight—your gift from me!

Take the poppet outside, and tie the ends of the ribbon to a tree branch, saying:

Come little birds: Come one and all!
Hear me, hear me! Hear my call!
Eat this treat I've made for you,
Pick the seeds out through and through,
And when you've pecked the seeds away,
Peck the flesh until the day

That (name of target) *has paid the full amount*
That's owed to me without discount,
And only then, you'll let him/her be
And end this pecking misery!

Walk away and let the birds do their thing.

Eye on the Debt Hex

Materials:

> *1 peacock feather*
> *Commanding/Controlling/Compelling Powder*
> *Paper bag*
> *Stapler*

Write the target's name on the paper bag, then clip the "eye" portion from the rest of the feather and place it inside, sprinkling it liberally with the powder. Fold the top of the bag three times to close, and staple it shut with nine staples. Now, give the bag a good shake to engage the "mind's eye" in the target's brain, and say:

Your mind's eye has just engaged,
And now on you, a war it's waged.
Reminding that you owe me cash
With every blink and every flash.
Nothing else does it let you see,
Its vision haunts you constantly.
Insisting that you pay me now,
Insisting that you not allow

This debt to go on any longer,
When you resist, it just gets stronger.
Pursuing you relentlessly
Until you write a check to me
And clear this up, you'll not be free.
Pay me now or pay the price:
A curse of sleepless days and nights!

Bury the bag close to your mailbox.

Legal Debt Collection

If the money owed you is a legal debt of sorts—a court settlement, child support, or payment bound by contract—send an envelope of courthouse dirt to the deadbeat in question. Do not include a return address.

Enemies

Five-Minute Cigarette Hex

WARNING: this hex may cause illness in the target!

Materials:

> *1 cigarette*
> *Black pen*
> *Lighter or matches*

Write the target's full name on the cigarette, then light and smoke it while seeing the offender being burned from your life. As you smoke, say something like:

From my life, you are now burned.
You wisp away, just so much smoke
From my life, you fall like ash
The remnants of a Cosmic joke.

When you've finished, put out the cigarette, and squeeze out any remaining tobacco. Discard the butt in a public trash receptacle.

Get Out of My Life Hex

As this spell is extremely difficult to reverse, be absolutely certain that you want the target out of your life completely and forever before using it.

Materials:

> *Prepared poppet*
> *1 black candle*
> *3 to 4 tablespoons patchouli*
> *Black electrical tape or ribbon*
> *Graveyard dirt (see Chapter 2)*
> *Small piece of black onyx*
> *Salt*
> *Charcoal block*
> *Cigarette carton or a box large enough to fit the poppet*

Begin by lighting the candle and charcoal block. When the charcoal is ready, sprinkle it liberally with the patchouli, and pass the poppet through the smoke. Starting at the top of the head and working toward the feet, use a length of tape or ribbon to bind the poppet good and tight with a crisscrossing motion while saying:

Your interference in my life
Stops right now, as does the strife
You've caused for me by word and deed.
I bind it so it can't reseed.
Your influence, too, is bound up tight
And has no effect upon my life.
So what you say and what you do
Only circle back on you.
I bind the harm you've sought to cause,
I bind the troubles that it draws,
I bind them strong and tight to you,
So they can't touch me—no matter what you do.

Place the poppet in the box, and sprinkle it with graveyard dirt, saying:

With graveyard dirt, I defend my life
From any damage, stress, or strife
You wish to cause from here on out
For me, or those I care about.
With graveyard dirt, I defend my name
And honor, and I now regain
My reputation and appeal—
The very things you sought to steal.

Add the black onyx to the box, saying:

I add black onyx to this spell
To separate us and dispel
Any further action on your part
To screw with me, my life, or heart.

Sprinkle the contents of the box with salt, saying:

And with this salt, I take control,
I take your power from my soul.
I extricate myself from you,
And all your harm I now undo.

Finish filling the box with graveyard dirt, and seal it securely with electrical tape. Place the box in front of the candle and say:

And as this wax does melt away
So does your hold on me this day.
You've never been a friend of mine,
And now my back is turned in kind.
The bottom line is this, m'dear,
You only have yourself to fear.
For I have bound your shit to you,
And if you so much as dare to screw
With me again, that day you'll rue,
For all the magic that you do
Will immediately crash right down on you!

Leave the box in front of the candle until it burns out, then bury the box outside or place it in your freezer.

Financial Ruin

Empty Wallet Hex

Materials:

> *New wallet*
> *1 black candle*
> *Mechanical pencil or stylus*

To sentence your enemy to a life of poverty and financial ruin, purchase a new wallet to give to the target as a gift. Empty the wallet of everything except the identification card and set aside.

Using the pencil or stylus, inscribe the candle with the name of your target. Carve a dollar sign beneath the name, and draw a large X through it. Light the candle and pass the wallet through the flame nine times while visualizing the target. Then, still holding it in your hands, say:

> *With an empty wallet and empty purse*
> *You, (name of target), I hereby curse:*
> *For as long as you shall live,*
> *Your cash flows out as through a sieve.*
> *Poor as a church mouse you shall be:*
> *Cursed in money, cursed by me!*

Leave the wallet in front of the candle until the wick burns out. Then gift wrap the wallet, and present it to your enemy.

Anthill Hex

To create financial discord, sprinkle the target's doorstep with dirt from an anthill.

Gossip, Lies, and General Diarrhea of the Mouth

Pants Afire Spell

Use to curse a liar and to expose his or her lies to the rest of the world.

Materials:

> *1 new pair underwear related to the gender of the target*
> *Black permanent marker*
> *1 teaspoon black pepper*
> *1 cotton ball*
> *Rubbing alcohol*
> *Hot sauce*
> *A few thorns, thistles, nettles, or sticker burs*
> *Length of black ribbon or yarn*
> *Cauldron or fireproof container*

Using the black marker, write the target's name in the crotch area of the underwear. Sprinkle the area liberally with hot sauce, then add the pepper and thorns. Add a few drops of rubbing alcohol to the cotton ball and place it on top. Now fold the underwear several times to secure the ingredients, and tie the bundle tightly with the black yarn or ribbon.

Place the bundle in the cauldron or fireproof container, and set it on fire, chanting as it burns:

Liar, liar, pants on fire!
Tongue that wags, add to the pyre!
With this flame that licks and lights,
The truth shall come forth pure and bright.
The world shall see you as you are:
Spreading lies both near and far,
I have had enough of you
And this curse, you can't undo:
Every time you start to lie
Your ass will burn, your eyes will cry;
Your tongue will still inside your lips
Each and every time you slip.
Only when you tell what's true
Shall this curse not bother you!

When the ashes are cool, scatter them in an open field or at a crossroads.

Gossip Gagging Hex

Materials:

> *Photograph or likeness of the target (Draw*
>   *a simple face if you have to.)*
> *Black thread*
> *Sharp needle*

Thread the needle and use it to sew the lips of the likeness together with a series of cross-stitches. As you sew, chant:

Your lips are sealed and cannot spew
Gossip like they used to do.
No more talking out of turn,
No more pretending mere concern,
No more wagging of your tongue,
Nor babble from your mouth be sprung.
Sewn and gagged, your lips stay still
Both day and night as I do will.

Fold the likeness in half twice, and stitch the edges closed. When you've finished, either bury it as close to the target's property as possible or in a pot of dirt outside your home.

Matters of the Heart

To Bring Back an Errant Lover

Materials:

> *1 tablespoon mistletoe*
> *Red bag with drawstring closure*
> *Red pen*
> *Paper*

Using the red pen, draw two intersecting hearts on the paper. Write your name on one heart and your lover's on the other. Sprinkle the mistletoe over the hearts, then fold the paper in half twice, and place in the bag. Close the bag securely, and tie the ends together six times. Hide the bag in your lover's bedroom or workplace. Results usually come within nine days.

Panties in a Knot Binding

Materials:

> *1 pair of your underwear*
> *1 pair of your intended's underwear*
> *6 drops Oshun Oil*

On the night of the Full Moon, fold each pair of underwear into a rectangle. Place one rectangle in front of you vertically and the other across it horizontally to form a cross. Knot the ends of the pair on the bottom around the pair on the top, then flip the structure over, and repeat the process. Place three drops of Oshun Oil on each knot, saying with each drop:

> *Oh, Goddess of Love! Oh, Lovely Oshun!*
> *Lend your power and strength to this magical Moon,*
> *And use it to bind our hearts as one,*
> *And our bodies as well. As I will, be it done!*

Place the binding beneath your mattress, or hide it in the drawer with your underwear.

To Keep a Lover from Straying

Materials:

> *1 hat pin or doll needle (readily available at*
> *your local arts and crafts store)*

Use the pin to draw a heart in the center of your lover's footprint. Then stab the heart six times, saying with each insertion:

> *With me, you shall stay*
> *And never slip away.*

By this design
You shall be mine,
And never shall you stray.

Scrape up a little dirt from the footprint, and scatter it under your bed.

Stray No More Spell

To keep a lover from straying, bury a photograph of him or her facedown in your yard with the head pointing toward the house.

To Obtain the Love of a Specific Person
(Even if they're already taken!)

Materials:

> *Poppet fashioned in your likeness*
> *Poppet fashioned in the target's likeness*
> *1 red candle*
> *1 pink candle*
> *1 tablespoon each rosemary, cloves, cinnamon,*
> *   rose petals, basil, and ginger*
> *Queen Bitch Oil*
> *Scarlet ribbon*
> *¼ yard red velvet*

Mix the herbs together well, and divide between the body cavities of each poppet, using cotton to secure in place if necessary. Add six drops of Queen Bitch Oil to the body cavities of the target poppet. (Do NOT add this to the doll representing you!)

Run a flame up the side of one candle, press it against the other candle to hold them together, and light both wicks. Then secure the poppets together face-to-face with the scarlet ribbons by wrapping them in crisscross fashion. As you wrap, chant:

Herbs of love and hot desire

Set (name of target)'s heart and loins afire.

Fire of love and sex and passion,

Light (name of target)'s heart—jolt him/her into action.

Tied hand to hand and heart to heart,

We shall be and never part.

And all his/her love s/he'll bring to me,

As I will, so mote it be.

Secure the ribbon wrapping by tying a bow, and place in front of the candles until they burn out. Wrap the dolls in the red velvet and place beneath your bed.

Love Potion #9

Materials:

> *1 ounce vodka*
> *1 ounce bourbon*
> *1 ounce sloe gin*
> *1 tablespoon Galliano*
> *Orange juice*
> *3 maraschino cherries*

Fill a tall glass half-full with ice, and pour in the vodka, bourbon, and sloe gin. Finish filling with orange juice, stir well, and say:

Burning passion! Fiery lust!

Infuse this potion with your thrust,

So that s/he who drinks it shall desire

To pleasure me and then aspire
To keep it up 'til satisfaction
I have reached; and let attraction
Fuel things further with romance;
Aid me in this lusty dance.

Float the Galliano on the top of the mixture, then add the cherries one by one, saying:

Cherries, sweetly kiss this drink
And bring (name of target) *past the brink*
Of only lust. Engage his/her heart—
Pierce it as the Cupid's dart—
So that s/he falls in love with me
Sweetly, madly, and passionately.

Serve the drink to the object of your intent.

Lady Dame's Ex Hex

Use this hex when an ex-spouse has done you dirty and needs to be taught a lesson.

Materials:

Mad Oil
Your wedding ring
Dirt from the home you shared together (Substitute
    dirt from your current home if necessary.)
1 small wooden box (A lightweight box is best.)
1 lancet or sharp, sterile needle
Paper and pen
Fireproof container (Use the fireplace instead if you have one.)

Place the dirt in the box, saturate it with Mad Oil, and set it aside to soak. Now write down everything you've ever wanted to say to your ex-spouse. Recount every hurt, every tear, every misery. Recount all the pain s/he caused and all the anger you felt. But don't stop there. Be sure to tell the ex what a genuine jackass s/he is and how s/he's not even fit to eat with pigs. Don't stop until you've gotten it all down.

When you're done, place your wedding ring on top of the paper, and fold it into a packet so that the writing and the ring are on the inside. Then, using the lancet or needle, prick your finger, and drip three drops of blood onto the packet. Place the packet in the box on top of the soil and say:

From the day we met, love grew and bloomed,
It filled our hearts, it filled our room,
But now our time has come and gone,
And you will be the one alone!

Place the box in the fireproof container or fireplace, and set it on fire. When the box and its contents are reduced to ash, either let the ring cool and mail it to your ex, or toss the ring and ashes into a river and wash the mess out of your life.

Erectile Dysfunction Hex

Materials:

> Length of red cord or ribbon

Measure your lover's penis, and cut the cord length to the measurement. Starting at the center of the cord, tie nine equidistant knots, saying with each one:

With this knot to me you're tied,
Only for me shall you rise,
Only for me shall you grow,
And if wild oats you try to sow,
Limp and flaccid you shall be
Until you come back home to me.

Carry the cord with you at all times, and your lover won't be able to perform with anyone but you.

Faithful Female Spell

Materials:

> High John the Conqueror root
> Sugar
> Cayenne pepper
> Coffee grinder

Set the coffee grinder to fine, then dump in the ingredients, and blend for ten to fifteen seconds. Sprinkle a bit of the powder around your lover's bed, and toss the rest beneath it, saying over and over:

Sure as on two feet you stand
Your faithfulness I now command,
You cannot cheat—you cannot stray—you're true to me
> *both night and day.*

Payback Time

Yemaya's Fish Dinner Hex

Materials:

> *1 whole fish*
> *Cane syrup (Be sure this is made from sugar cane and*
> *   is not corn syrup! If cane syrup is not available*
> *   in your area, substitute white cane sugar.)*
> *Plastic container with a snap-on lid large*
> *   enough to accommodate the fish*
> *Black pen*
> *Paper*
> *7 straight pins (If using pins with colored*
> *   heads, use blue and white only.)*
> *7 dimes*

Using the black pen, make a list of all your enemies and stuff it in the fish's mouth. Add the dimes and pin it closed securely. Pour enough cane syrup or sugar over the fish to coat it well, then offer it to Yemaya, saying:

> *Yemaya, I call on You*
> *To bring these folks what they have due.*
> *Their just desserts is what I ask,*
> *Yemaya, take them all to task.*
> *And as a gift to seal the deal,*
> *I offer You this lovely meal.*

Snap the lid onto the container, and repeat the request to Yemaya each day for seven days. On the eighth day, remove the fish from the container—yeah . . . it's going to smell awful—throw it into the ocean, and blow a kiss to Yemaya. (If you don't live in close proximity to the sea, sprinkle the fish with a handful of salt, and dispose of it in a body of fresh water.)

Full Circle Curse

Hold your right arm above your head with your index finger pointing upward, and move it counterclockwise in a circular motion while chanting:

> *I vow before this day is done*
> *Before the setting of the Sun*
> *That all you say and all you do*
> *Will fly directly back at you.*
> *And all that hurt and all that pain*
> *And all the anguish they contains*
> *Shall rain on you like pelting hail*
> *And take you down by forceful gale.*

Hex of the Nine-Patch

Materials:

> *Black pen*
> *Black skull candle*
> *Black ribbon or yarn*
> *Fireproof dish*
> *Letter-size sheet of paper*

Place the candle in the dish, and light it while thinking of how much misery your enemy has caused you. Draw the nine-patch on the paper (see illustration below).

Then write your target's name three times across each horizontal row of squares. Visualize your enemy's every effort coming to naught, and see his or her power waning. Then say:

I take the things you've done to me
And return them to you at three times three.
Nine times the agony, nine times the pain,
Nine times the misery, nine times the bane,
Nine times worse than you've ever known,
Feel nine times the horror right down in your bones.
Feel nine times more weakness than you've ever felt,
Feel nine times more sickness than you've ever dealt.
Feel nine times more wretched for sowing the seeds
That brought on this hex and your harvest of weeds.
Your every attempt comes to naught with this spell,
Your efforts are useless—not a thing turns out well—
By this patch of nine, numbered three squares by three,
Your fate is now sealed. As I will, it shall be!

Place the sheet of paper in front of the dish, and leave it there until the candle extinguishes itself. Then scrape any leftover wax onto the paper. Fold the paper into thirds, then into thirds again, and secure it with the black ribbon or yarn by tying the ends into nine knots.

When you've finished preparing the packet, bury it in the ground—preferably on your target's property or as close to that property as possible. If burying it isn't a possibility but gaining access to your target's property is, hide it among their possessions. Possibilities might include hiding it under the doormat, in a potted plant, behind a piece of furniture, or in a desk drawer.

To Fix a Troublemaker

Materials:

> *1 large lime*
> *2 nails*
> *Pen and paper*
> *White vinegar*
> *Salt*
> *Matches or lighter*
> *Cauldron or fireproof dish*
> *Scissors*
> *Jar with a tight-fitting, screw-on lid*

Write the target's name on the paper, cut it out close to the lettering, then burn the rest of the paper to ash in the cauldron or fireproof dish. While the ashes cool, score the lime into quarters, cutting the fruit about three-quarters of the way through. Fold the name in half twice, and insert it deeply into the lime, saying:

> *Your antics and your tricks go sour,*
> *Starting now: this very hour.*

Pin the lime sections securely with the nails to form an X, saying:

X marks the spot where you are held
And all the trouble you have spelled
For me is trapped along with you
No matter what you try to do.

Drop the lime into the jar, then dump the ashes and a handful of salt on top, saying:

I thwart your efforts—all shall fail—
By salt and ash and lime and nail.

Cover the mixture with vinegar, and say:

With vinegar, I complete this mix,

Finally, screw the lid on tightly and say:

And seal you in: This trick is fixed.

Shake the jar enough times to blend the mixture thoroughly, then place the jar on a dark shelf in your home.

IRS Audit Hex

Rather than being designed to exact permanent damage, this hex is geared more toward keeping the target busy enough to stay out of your life and stop interfering in your business!

Materials:

1 orange candle
Queen Bitch Oil
Page 1 of the current Form 1040 (download it from: www.irs.gov)
Red marker
Pen

Download and print the form, then add the target's name and address in the appropriate places. (If you don't have the target's complete address, that's all right. Just add the city and state information.) Now write FULL AUDIT across the form in large capital letters with the red marker.

Anoint the candle with the oil, and place it securely in a candleholder. Place the form face up in front of you and the candle in the center of it saying:

(Name of target), *you haven't had enough to do*
And interfered in things that you
Had no business messing in
So now your busy time begins:
With an audit, you are blessed
With five returns or more accessed.
You have time for nothing more
With IRS folks at your door,
Breathing down your neck all day,
Wanting proof and stubs of pay,
Asking for receipts for those
Deductions and those gifts bestowed.
A full audit for (name of target), *I demand,*
Spirits, act on this command.
Bring this audit immediately,
I will it, want it—and it shall be.

Leave the form where it is until the candlewick burns out, then bury or hide it in close proximity to the IRS office or a building where taxes are collected. (If you don't have a local IRS office, good alternatives are the local tax assessor's office or courthouse.)

Pins and Needles

While the use of poppets was covered in Chapter 3, pin and needle insertions in conjunction with their use was not. Of course, if the intent is to cause illness, locating the proper insertion point is just a matter of common sense. However, other key insertion points are often overlooked. And it's to that end that a brief list follows below for your convenience.

Mouth: To keep someone from spreading lies, speaking ill of you, or to hold gossip at bay, insert nine pins in the mouth.

Buttocks: To keep someone from taking your job, place three pins in each buttock cheek.

Hands: Insert pins here to keep the target from stealing from you—this could include preventing the theft of your lover—and to sentence him or her to a life of poverty.

Head: Pins inserted in this area can cause confusion, disorientation, and depression.

Eyes: These are excellent insertion points when the intent involves making the target oblivious to your actions.

Nose: Insert two pins in each nostril to stop nosy neighbors, or keep the target from interfering in your business.

Power Removal

The One Shot Spell

(Note: do not use rum for this spell! As it is sacred to some of the Afro-Caribbean deities, using it as such may be offensive to Them.)

Materials:

> *1 shot of vodka, bourbon, gin, or scotch*
> *1 glass to hold the shot of alcohol*
> *1 12-ounce glass of water*

Pour the shot of alcohol, then swirl it in the glass, saying:

> (Name of target) *you've become*
> (Name of target) *you shall stay*
> *And I've become the nemesis*
> *Who will take your power away.*

Take a sip from the glass, saying:

> *One sip and you feel weak,*

Take another sip, saying:

> *Another makes you fall.*

Then chug the rest of the shot and say:

> *As I toss back the rest of this*
> *I own your power: All!*

Now chase the shot with the full glass of water, drinking it down as quickly as possible. Then say:

In an hour's time, I'll piss you out
And you'll be laid to waste,
Weak and lowly like the piss
And swimming in disgrace.

To Relieve Your Enemy of Personal Power

Please be aware that this spell not only has the capacity to relieve the target's power over you, but also drains his or her personal power. That being the case, the target may also become physically ill or experience a nasty bout of depression.

Materials:

> *Poppet*
> *9 corsage pins or other large pins*
> *3 to 4 tablespoons patchouli*
> *Black candle drippings*
> *Target's taglock (see Taglocks section for ideas)*
> *Box large enough to accommodate the poppet*

On the first day of the New Moon, stick the pins into the poppet in a straight line from the head to the crotch, then work down each leg to the feet. With each pin, say:

With this pin, I prick your power,
It starts to ooze this very hour,
It bleeds and ebbs and drains away,
'Til it's as gone as yesterday.

When the last pin is in place, put the poppet in the box, and place the taglock on top. Sprinkle well with patchouli, and seal the box with black candle drippings. Bury the box at sunset.

Protective Measures

Anyone who performs hexes and curses would be a fool not to go the extra mile to protect themselves against the same. Thus, the following protection ideas are provided for your convenience.

Against the Evil Eye:

- Hang dill weed over all windows and doorways in the home.

- Wear a blue eye bead for constant personal protection. Hang one from the rearview mirror of your car, as well.

- Keep a cimaruta (an Italian talisman sporting multiple symbols) on your altar to stave off interference in your magical work.

Against Nightmares:

- Keep a silver bell in your bedroom, and ring it to drive off nightmare-causing evil spirits each night before you go to bed.

- A small dish of coffee beans kept by the bed staves off nightmares.

- Rosemary plants placed near the bed shield against unpleasant dreams.

For Safe Automobile Travel:

- Keep a whole ash leaf in the glove box for magical protection.

- Keep a tiger's eye in the vehicle to protect against accidents.

- Hang a mojo bag filled with wormwood and plantain from the rearview mirror to prevent negative spirits from taking on the position of copilot.

Against Malevolence in the Home:

- Once a month, use a sprig of rosemary to asperge all thresholds with a mixture of 1 tablespoon of saltpeter to a gallon of water. Pay special attention to the front and back doors.

- Place aloe vera plants above the doorway to repel malevolent spirits and nasty magic. Use red geraniums outdoors—if your property allows it, plant them to form a boundary—to keep bewitchments at bay.

- Place Fu dog statues—the Asian dogs that look as if they're part lion—on either side of the front door as "security guards." It's said that using a matched pair of male and female is most effective. (The male is usually portrayed playing with a ball.) Raise them off the ground as much as possible, so they can get a clear view of anything coming their way.

- As Papa Legba holds the keys to the gates between the worlds and decides who enters and who doesn't, place his statue behind the front door. (A statue of St. Peter may be substituted, as he was designated by the enslaved as Papa Legba's Christian counterpart when it was necessary to hide their religious activities.) Offer him rum every Monday—Barbancourt is a good choice if you can find it—and occasionally supplement with good cigars, cigarettes, and candy.

Against Pet Harm:

- As pets take the brunt of any malicious activity aimed toward us, it's important to safeguard them as well. For dogs, a disc depicting Diana and charged with protection works well when added to the collar. For cats, obtain a disc depicting Bast. If neither is available to you, a St. Francis of Assisi medal will work well for either.

Relocation

To Make an Enemy Move

This spell is also useful in forcing a coworker to quit his or her job or find another.

Materials:

> *Small bottle with a tight-fitting screw-on lid*
> *(Soy sauce bottles work well for this.)*
> *Four Thieves Vinegar*
> *Pen and paper*

Write your enemy's name nine times on a piece of paper, and place in the bottle. Add enough Four Thieves Vinegar to completely cover the paper, then cap tightly, and toss into a river.

Mary Caliendo's Enemy-Removal Spell

This spell will completely rid you of any enemies. (As they just seem to disappear into the ether, I take a "don't ask" stance with this one!)

> *1 potato*
> *Black permanent marker*
> *White glue*
> *Black glitter*
> *Paintbrush (optional)*

Write the name of your enemy on the potato with the marker, then cover it with glue. (A paintbrush makes short work of this.) Then roll the potato in black glitter and bury it.

Nasty Neighbor Spell

Materials:

> *Your morning urine*
> *9 black peppercorns*
> *3 tablespoons salt*
> *1 clove garlic, peeled*
> *3 rusty nails*
> *Jar with tight-fitting screw-on lid*

Place all ingredients in the jar, screw on the lid, and shake it continuously while chanting:

> *I piss on you and all you've done,*
> *Pack your things—get out now—run!*
> *Your place—that house and property—*
> *Is no longer yours, you see,*
> *You may not live there anymore*
> *On you, it has shut its door.*
> *I'm done with you, and with this mix*
> *A moving trick on you I'll fix.*

Throw the contents of the jar in the neighbor's yard and mutter under your breath:

> *I mark you now with piss and rust,*
> *With garlic, pepper, and salty crust.*
> *Pack your things and leave today.*
> *This trick is fixed. Now go away!*

Walk away and don't look back.

Black Candle Banishing

Materials:

> 1 black candle
> Patchouli oil
> Mechanical pencil or stylus

Using the mechanical pencil, mark the candle into three equal portions. Then starting at the bottom of the candle and working upward (away from you) inscribe the target's name three times. When you are finished, anoint the candle with patchouli oil. Burn one-third of the candle on each of three consecutive days, saying each time you light it:

> *Go away! Far away!*
> *Close to me, you cannot stay!*
> *Run away! Far away!*
> *Pack your things and leave today!*

Make Tracks Spell

To force a nasty neighbor to move, mix together equal amounts of graveyard dirt and Hot Foot Powder, and toss into the target's yard on nine consecutive nights. Moving arrangements should be in progress by the tenth day.

Greeting Card Spell

To remove an enemy from your life, send him or her a greeting card that you've anointed with patchouli oil.

Revenge

Chicken Bone Curse

Materials:

> *2 chicken bones of equal length*
> *1 skein black embroidery floss*

Cut the floss into three equal lengths. Then holding the bones together to form an equal-armed cross, bind them together with the first length in a crisscrossing motion. As you bind the bones, think of your target, and chant the following over and over:

> *You shall eat from the same plate*
> *As that from which you serve your guests.*

When you reach the last inch, tie one knot in the front and a knot in the back. Repeat the process with the other two lengths of floss. Throw the fetish in the target's yard, or hide it on the property.

Element Curse

Materials:

> *Red marker*
> *Black pen*
> *Paper*
> *Crossing Incense*
> *Cauldron or fireproof dish*

Using the black pen, write the following on the paper.

> *I summon You, Elements! Come to me, All:*
> *Air, Fire, Water, and Earth, I call!*
> *I have been wronged and I conjure You*
> *To swiftly bring justice for all I've been through*
> *To the one who has wrought all my anguish and pain*
> *I demand that the following on his/her head do rain:*
> *One hundred times over, the problems s/he's caused,*
> *One hundred times over with nary a pause*
> *The fear, pain, and anguish, one hundred times too*
> *Without mercy or pity, give him/her what is due.*
> *I command misery and I command guilt.*
> *I command s/he receives what s/he's wrought and s/he's built.*
> *I conjure You, Elements! Do as I say!*
> *Carry out my demands before the end of this day!*

When you've finished writing, use the red marker to write the target's name over the incantation. (Do this in large letters in a vertical line from top to bottom in the center of the paper.)

Hold the paper in your hands, and recite the curse with force and feeling. Then sprinkle the paper with Crossing Incense, fold it into thirds, and set it on fire, saying:

You are thus cursed
Your fate is thus sealed,
There's no going back
And no way to shield.
Cursed by the Earth, the Fire, Wind, and Sea
Cursed by all Four—and cursed, too, by me!

When the ashes are cool, flush them down the toilet.

Graveyard Curse

This curse depends upon easy access to the grave of a relative or someone who would care deeply about your plight.

Materials:

Pen and paper
Gift for the deceased

Sit down and write the deceased a letter explaining your troubles and precisely what you'd like done about them. Be explicit with your instructions, and don't leave anything out. Above all, don't leave anything up to the spirit of the deceased, as doing so is likely to bring results other than those you desire.

When you're finished, take the letter and the gift to the gravesite. Read the letter to the spirit of the deceased, and mention that you've brought a gift in payment for its help. Dig a shallow hole in the general proximity of the place you'd expect the deceased's right hand to be. Bury both objects in the hole, thank the spirit, and leave the cemetery without looking back.

Separation

To End a Relationship

Materials:

> *1 egg*
> *1 to 2 tablespoons slippery elm*
> *Sheet of paper*
> *Red pen*
> *Black yarn or embroidery floss*

Carefully break the egg, and feed it to a dog or other animal. (You may also feed it to another person, if necessary, but do NOT eat the egg yourself. Although the egg won't harm anyone, it's imperative that you not connect yourself to the magic in this fashion.) Fill both halves of the eggshell with slippery elm, then put them back together, and bind well with the yarn or floss. Tie three knots to secure. Then using the red pen, write the following on the paper:

> *As Sun from Moon, and Day from Night,*
> *As Mountain from Valley, and Land from Sea,*
> *As Earth from Sky, and Dark from Light,*
> *As He from She, and I from We,*
> *So separate, sever, and divide*
> (Name of one person) *from* (name of the other person).
> *Separate them far and wide*
> *From each other, make them part*
> *Without a care in either's heart.*

Wrap the egg in the paper, making sure that the writing is on the inside. Bury the parcel as close to the couple's home as possible.

Black Onyx Separation

To separate a couple, present one of the parties with a piece of black onyx.

Sexual Harassment

Spell to Stop Sexual Harassment

Materials:

> *A copy of the Devil card from the Tarot*
> *Black candle*
> *Red permanent marker*
> *Black permanent marker*
> *Saltpeter*
> *Small dish of ice water*
> *Small paintbrush*

Light the candle on a Saturday between 11:00 a.m. and 1:00 p.m., place the copy of the card in front of it, and call the target to mind. See all the trouble s/he's caused in minute detail. Feel the discomfort you've experienced, and let it envelope you. Now get pissed and work yourself up into a wall-eyed fit. Once you've worked yourself up into a state of real fury, write the target's name in red across the face of the card copy. Using the black marker, outline the card margins, and draw vertical bars through the image like the bars of a cage. Chant:

I confine you now by chain and bar—
Just like the animal that you are—
You've been snared and all can see
Your true colors perfectly.
And caught within this trap of might
All you've done now comes to light.
(A fitting place for you to be
On view without your dignity!)
I curse you by the law of land
And from the Spirits, I demand
Curses of another kind,
The terms of which I now define:

At this point, wet the paintbrush with ice water and dip it into the saltpeter. If the card copy contains an image of the appropriate gender, use the brush to paint the genital area. If not, paint an X through the entire card. Say:

From this day forward you shall be
The victim of impotency.
There'll be no cure and no release,
The problem shall not ever cease.
And further, I demand that They
Remove your power from this day,
And see to it you'll never fill
A position where your personal will
Can harm or injure or coerce,
By these terms, you are now cursed!

Fold the card copy neatly as many times as is possible, and leave it in front of the candle until the wick burns out. If the target is a coworker, hide the card as close to his or her office as possible. If not, carry the card with you.

Condom Hex

Materials:

> *1 condom*
> *1 rusty nail (Substitute a thorn, if necessary.)*
> *Salt*
> *Black pepper*
> *Black permanent marker*

Unwrap the condom, place it in front of you, and write the target's name on it. Then visualize the target wearing the condom, and using the nail or thorn, stab it repeatedly while saying:

> *I prick you where it hurts the most*
> *In your pathetic little host,*

Sprinkle it with salt, saying:

> *I salt the wounds so that they sting*
> *Each time you try to use that thing.*

Now, blacken the condom with pepper, saying:

> *And now, I set a penile fire*
> *So when you're hardened by desire,*
> *It burns like hell without relief*
> *Then shrivels up within your briefs,*
> *And all that's left upon your mind*
> *Is how to cool your burning tine.*

Place the nail or thorn inside the condom, and secure it with a knot. Dispose of the condom in a public trash receptacle.

Bergamot Preventative

Wear bergamot oil as a perfume to prevent being the object of sexual harassment.

Sleep Disorders

Nightmare-Inducing Dream Catcher

Materials:

> *5-inch metal ring*
> *4 yards ⅛" suede lacing*
> *4 yards imitation sinew (flat waxed thread)*
> *Bead or stone with a hole in it*
> *Clothespin*
> *White glue*

Glue one end of the lacing to the ring and secure it with the clothespin. Then, moving counterclockwise, wrap the lacing tightly around the ring until you reach the starting point. Cut the lacing, glue the end, and secure it with the clothespin as well.

Tie one end of the thread to the ring, and moving counter-clockwise, tie nine evenly spaced half hitches around the perimeter. (To tie a half hitch, bring the thread over the top of the ring and behind it, pulling it over the loop formed by the length of thread stretched between the current knot and the previous one.) Tie the last half hitch approximately a half inch before the starting point.

Continuing to work in a counterclockwise direction, tie a half hitch in the center of each stitch from the previous round.

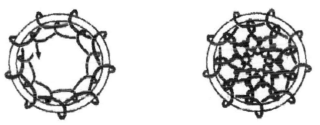

Repeat the process with each round until you reach the center of the web, then add the bead and tie off. Then enchant the dream catcher by saying:

> *Your dreams shall haunt you every night*
> *Until your sleep is fraught with fright.*
> *Of what you've done to cause me harm,*

Your chest shall pound in pure alarm.
You'll sweat and shake in terror through
Each night until I get my due.
Until you finally make amends,
Your restful nights are at an end.

Restless Spirits Curse

Materials:

9 dimes

Hold the dimes in your hand, and visualize the target being the object of spirit aggravation. Say:

All restless Spirits, I do call
Who roam the Earth when night does fall
To (name of target) *do go and cause unrest,*
Leave him/her in wild distress.
Without a wink of sleep in sight
And every minute fraught with fright,
With frazzled nerves and sheer dismay
And for this service, I do pay
These dimes to cut our own connection
And guarantee your clear direction.

Toss the nine dimes at a crossroads away from your home to prevent the Spirits from disturbing your sleep as well.

No Rest for the Wicked Hex

Materials:

> 1 black feather
> 1 tablespoon valerian
> Small red bag with drawstring

Place the feather and valerian in the bag, draw up the ends, and knot them nine times. Hang the bag over the target's bedroom door.

As long as the bag stays in place, no one will be able to rest or dream peacefully in that room.

Taglocks

While snippets of hair or fingernail clippings are most widely used to connect magic to a target, other taglocks can be used just as effectively in their place. The following list comprises some great substitutions that are much more easily obtained.

- Butt from a cigarette smoked by the target

- Discarded gum chewed by the target

- Tissue used to blow the target's nose

- Tissue used to wipe the target's glasses

- Paper towel used to wipe the target's hands

- Paper napkin used to wipe the target's mouth

- Plastic knife, fork, or spoon used by the target

- Paper or plastic drinking cup used by the target

- Paper crumpled and discarded by the target

- Dirt from the target's footprint

Torment, Irritation, and General Aggravation

Public Coffin Hex

This is probably the easiest—and most famous—curse in this entire book, as it requires nothing more of you than putting the parcel together and seeing to delivery. Because of its ability to frighten and terrify, the target actually winds up cursing him or herself!

Materials:

> *Small wooden box (For full impact, try to*
> *find one shaped like a coffin.)*
> *1 raw chicken liver, split in half lengthwise*
> *13 straight pins*
> *Graveyard dirt (optional)*
> *Pen and paper*

Write the target's name on the paper, and insert between the two liver halves. Pin in place securely with the straight pins, then sprinkle with graveyard dirt if you like. Close the box, place it on the target's front doorstep, and watch the curse ensue.

Get Lost Hex

While this hex will definitely force the target to leave you alone, it also causes enough personal aggravation so that he or she is way too busy to bother anyone else.

Materials:

> *Prepared poppet*
> *Black wax, melted*
> *Lost and Away Powder*
> *Brown paper sack*

Place the poppet in the sack and sprinkle liberally with Lost and Away Powder, saying:

> *Lost and away from me you go*
> *As your life's sprinkled with troubles, problems and woe.*

Pour the melted wax on top of the poppet, and quickly douse with the powder again. (Do this before the wax sets up, as you want the powder to adhere to it.) As you sprinkle the powder, say:

> *Problems stick like black to crow*
> *Like melted wax they ooze and flow,*
> *And when you think they're finally done,*
> *More arrive with rise of Sun.*

Bury the poppet in an area easily accessible to you but away from your home. To keep the hex active, visit the grave once each week, and dust it with the powder.

Crossroads Curse

Materials:

> *1 black candle*
> *Photograph of the target*
> *Small bag with drawstring closure (Any color will do.)*
> *Graveyard dirt*
> *An assortment of sharp objects (needles, pins,*
> *nails, tacks, broken mirrors or glass, etc.)*

Place all the objects in front of the candle, and light the wick. Add the sharp objects to the charm bag, then holding the photograph in your hands, tell the target just how mad you are. Yell, scream, and curse, working yourself up into a real tizzy. Then rip the image to shreds, toss it into the bag, and add the dirt. Place the bag in front of the candle, saying:

Things that cut and poke and prick,
Do your job by flaming wick.
Graveyard dirt, do your job too
So no relief shall come unto
(Name of target).
Together, you shall irritate,
Torment, plague, and aggravate,
Until the time you are retrieved
And of your duties, so relieved.

Leave the bag in front of the candle until the wick burns out, then add any leftover wax or wick to the contents. Close the bag and knot securely, then bury it at a crossroads in a cemetery.

Guilty as Charged Hex

Materials:

> *1 to 2 fresh pansy blossoms*
> *Goofer Dust Powder*
> *Paper and pen*
> *Red charm bag with drawstring closure*

Write the target's name at the top of the paper as if you were writing him or her a note. Then copy the following curse onto the paper. (This must be in your own handwriting, so don't cheat and type it!)

For all the things that you have done,
The blame you've cast while taking none,
The things you've taken credit for
Although you sailed right out the door,
And didn't lift a finger toward
A single one, but claimed the reward.
That awful way you've treated me
As if it were my place to be
Your servant—fetching this and that,
Kissing your feet, putting up with your crap—
With this curse, I swear you'll pay,
And this misery starts today:
Guilt to cloud your morning Sun,
Guilt to haunt and mar your fun.
Guilt so dark and guilt so deep,
All you'll want to do is weep.
Guilt so heavy over all
Your despicable acts, you'll want to fall,
To your knees and beg me to
Forgive, forget, and exonerate you.
But that won't happen, so you'll pay
Each and every single day
By bending over backwards to
Do for me as I did for you;

Still, nothing will ever be enough
To assuage the guilt to which you're cuffed.

Sign your name, then take the pansy, and rub each line of words thoroughly with the petals. (Apply a little elbow grease, as the idea is to get some of the juice on the paper.) Place what's left of the blossoms on top of the paper, sprinkle well with Goofer Dust, and spit on it three times.

Fold the paper to hold the contents, then continue to fold it until it's impossible to fold it again. Place it in the bag, pull the drawstrings shut, and secure with three knots. Bury the bag as close to the target's property as possible.

Witch's Bottle Hex

Materials:

> *13 straight pins*
> *3" x 3" square of red felt*
> *Black permanent marker*
> *Small bottle with a tight-fitting screw-on cap (Soy sauce*
> *and steak sauce bottles work well for this.)*
> *Assortment of sharp objects (broken glass, pins,*
> *needles, tacks, wood splinters, etc.)*
> *Black candle drippings*
> *Your urine*

Place the sharp objects in the bottle and set aside. Cut a heart from the felt, and write the target's name in the center. Then, one at a time, stab the pins through the heart in various locations, saying with each one:

I prick your heart and you shall bleed
With guilt for all your nasty deeds.

When all the pins are in place, put the heart in the bottle, and cover the contents with your urine. Drip black candle wax on the inside of the bottle cap and screw it on securely. Throw the bottle in the nearest river or some other body of running water.

Living Hell Hex

Materials:

> *1 black candle*
> *Four Thieves Vinegar*
> *Goofer Dust Powder*
> *Patchouli oil*
> *Pen and paper*
> *Cauldron or fireproof dish*

Soak the paper in the vinegar, allow to dry thoroughly, then write the target's name in the center. Anoint the candle with patchouli oil, sprinkle it lightly with Goofer Dust, and light the wick. Once the wick is burning steadily, light the paper from the flame, and toss it in the cauldron to burn. (Be sure this burns to ash; if it doesn't, relight it from the flame.)

After the candle burns out, sprinkle the ashes on the target's property.

Weeping Willow Hex

This hex brings bouts of tears and depression to the target's home.

Materials:

> *1 weeping willow branch (Do not cut a*
> *branch; find one on the ground.)*
> *Sharp knife*

5-gallon bucket
Pen and paper
Water

Using a sharp knife, cut the end of the branch at a sharp diagonal. Write the target's name on the paper, then spear it securely on the branch. Place the branch in the bucket, fill it with water, and say:

As the weeping willow cries
So shall tears fall from your eyes.
Despair and sadness shan't abate,
Misery shall be your fate.

Each day for nine days, add water to the bucket and repeat the chant. On the tenth day, remove the branch from the bucket and check for roots. If there are any, plant the branch away from your home; if not, throw the branch away. Toss the water on the target's front porch or lawn.

Vermin: Rats, Mice, Bedbugs, Etc.

Mary Caliendo's Vermin Hexing Spell

While this particular spell was initially created to eradicate mice and bedbugs, it may be easily reworked to handle any sort of vermin.

Materials:

1 black candle
Crossing Oil #2
Hot Foot Powder

1 garlic clove
⅛ teaspoon asafoetida
1 teaspoon Dragon's Blood
1 rusty nail
Vinegar
Jar with tight-fitting, screw-on lid
Your urine

Begin by saying:

Hecate and the Horned God entered my home
And saw that the vermin had started to roam.
They looked at the bedbugs, they picked up the mice,
Together we banished and cursed them right out of my life.
"The pests will now go," the Goddess, She said,
"And we'll start by banishing the bugs of the bed:
Curse them, curse them, 'til they are dead!"
Herne said, "The mice will find a new home
In the land of the dead, they will be free to roam,
Ganesha, forgive us if we've stepped on your toes.
Sacred are your mice, but they've become foes."

Anoint the candle with the oil and light the wick, saying:

This black candle will begin the curse,

Sprinkle Hot Foot Powder around the home while saying:

Three peppers mixed will make it disperse.

Place the jar in front of you, saying:

We'll bottle the evil so that it is cured,
And trauma and misery will become obscure.

Add the garlic to the jar, saying:

Garlic to exorcise its unholy light,

Add the asafoetida and say:

Asafoetida to curse it clear out of sight,

Add the Dragon's Blood, saying:

Dragon's Blood to add power and win the fight.

Add the rusty nail, saying:

A rusty nail to keep it at bay,

Fill the jar half full of vinegar, then urinate in it, saying:

Vinegar and piss to send it away.

Drip candle wax around the inside of the lid, then screw it tightly on the jar, saying:

Sealing the bottle with wax and so tight,
Will it I do and conclude this plight,
Never to return to cause me dismay—
Or rob me of energy by night or by day.
My home is once more filled with warm light
Sacred and safe and holy and bright!

Leave the jar in front of the candle until the wick burns out, then put it under your bed.

Workplace Woes

Mary Caliendo's Potato Chip Hex

This is so easy, you can perform it right at the office. Don't let its simplicity fool you, though. It's powerful enough to get rid of even the nastiest boss or coworker.

Materials:

> *2 bags potato chips (Get them from the building*
> *vending machine if possible.)*
> *3 packets black pepper*
> *1 sticky note*
> *Black pen*
> *Stapler*

Open both bags to let the air out. Write your enemy's name on the sticky note in black ink, place it in one of the bags, and add the pepper. Sit on the bag to crush the chips. (Move around a little if you need to, as it's imperative that the chips be reduced to crumbs.) Retrieve the bag, fold the top three times, and staple several times to secure. Place the bag in your purse, and toss it in a public garbage receptacle after work.

Now, eat the other bag of chips. You certainly wouldn't want to appear to be doing anything suspicious at work, would you?!

Mary Caliendo's Shredder Hex

Perfect for handling the nasty, condescending, and demanding tyrant who takes credit for your work to garner praise from the bosses, while you toil away unnoticed.

Materials:

> *Email from the target (the more patronizing and nasty the tone, the better)*

Print out the email, and draw a large black X across it from corner to corner. Now either put it in the shredder, or shred it with your bare hands while chanting:

> *What you do comes back to you*
> *With no escape and no rescue.*
> *Before this very day is through*
> *You shall rue the things you do.*

Wash your hands thoroughly to sever your connection to the target, then go on with your work. The problem will take care of itself before the end of the day.

Kiss Ass Curse

Materials:

> *1 black candle*
> *1 lemon*
> *3 coffin nails*
> *Graveyard dirt*
> *Pen and paper*

Light the candle, then cut the lemon in half lengthwise, being careful not to dislodge the seeds. Coat the inside of the fruit with graveyard dirt and set aside.

Write the target's name on the paper, and calling to mind all the things s/he's done to cause misery in the workplace, say:

Kiss ass, kiss ass, brown-nosed one,
You shall pay for what you've done.
All the blame that you have cast
On others comes back hard and fast.
All the credit that you took
Reels you in like fish on hook.
Honors that you stole and claimed
Are now declared and bring you shame.
While you were once the golden child,
Your reputation's now defiled.
Your two-faced crap is now revealed,
I've had enough—your fate is sealed—
I curse you with the seeds you've sown,
The harvest reaped shall be your own:
A ruinous harvest that's turned sour,
One that's reaped this very hour.

Drip candle wax across the name, then fold the paper. Drip more candle wax on the paper, and fold it again. Continue the process until the paper can no longer be folded. Then place it between the two lemon halves and, holding the fruit together, push a nail through its center to secure it. Push another nail through the fruit to the left side of the first, and drive the last one through to the right.

Place the lemon in front of the candle, and leave it there until the wick burns out. Bury the lemon.

White-Out Hex

Materials:

> Letter, memo, or email with the target's name on it
> Correction fluid
> Hot Foot Powder

Make a copy of the document, then white out the target's name everywhere it appears, saying with each erasure:

> *You,* (name of target), *I now erase:*
> *You're gone from this job and gone from this place.*

When the correction fluid is dry, rub a little Hot Foot Powder on each erasure and say:

> (Name of target), *make tracks and hit the road,*
> *Get out of here! You've been kayoed!*

Crumple up the paper, and deposit it in the trash receptacle nearest the target's work space.

Hagalaz Hex

To create general chaos for a boss or coworker, draw the Hagalaz rune on a piece of paper (see illustration below), and slip it among the papers on his or her desk. (This rune symbolizes hail and brings all sorts of chaos and misery.) Once the target picks it up and handles it—even if just to throw it in the trash—the rune has been "accepted." And once accepted, it begins to do its thing.

Bibliography

Bird, Stephanie Rose. *Sticks, Stones, Roots & Bones*. St. Paul, MN: Llewellyn Publications, 2004

Bivins, N. D. P. *Original Black and White Magic*. Los Angeles: International Imports, 1991

Canizares, Raul. *The Life and Works of Marie Laveau*. Plainview, NY: Original Publications, 2001

Carroll, William. *Superstitions: 10,000 You Really Need*. San Marcos, CA: Coda Publications, 1988

Cunningham, Scott. *Cunningham's Encyclopedia of Magical Herbs*. St. Paul, MN: Llewellyn Publications, 1986

Cunningham, Scott. *The Complete Book of Oils, Incenses, and Brews*. St. Paul, MN: Llewellyn Publications, 1989

Devine, M. V. *Brujería*. St. Paul, MN: Llewellyn Publications, 1982

Dorsey, Lilith. *Voodoo and Afro-Caribbean Paganism*. New York: Citadel Press, Inc., a division of Kensington Publishing Corp., 2005

Glassman, Sallie Ann. *Vodou Visions*. New York: Villard Books, a division of Random House, 2000

Gordon, Stuart. *The Book of Spells, Hexes, and Curses*. Secaucus, NJ: Citadel Press, a division of Carol Publishing Group, 1997

Hamilton, Edith. *Mythology—Timeless Tales of Gods and Heroes*. New York: Mentor Books, 1940

Haskins, Jim. *Voodoo & Hoodoo*. Plainview, NY: Original Publications, 1978

Illes, Judika. *The Element Encyclopedia of 5000 Spells*. London: Element, a division of HarperCollins Publishers, 2004

Kerenyi, Karl. *Goddesses of Sun and Moon*. Trans. Murray Stein. Dallas: Spring Publications, Inc., 1979

Lady Rhea and Eve LeFey. *The Enchanted Formulary*. New York: Citadel Press, Inc., a division of Kensington Publishing Corp., 2006

Malbrough, Ray T. *Charms, Spells & Formulas*. St. Paul, MN: Llewellyn Publications, 1986

Malbrough, Ray T. *Hoodoo Mysteries*. St. Paul, MN: Llewellyn Publications, 2003

Metraux, Alfred. *Voodoo in Haiti*. New York: Schocken Books, 1972

Monoghan, Patricia. *The New Book of Goddesses and Heroines*. St. Paul, MN: Llewellyn Publications, 1997

Monaghan, Patricia. *The Goddess Path*. St. Paul, MN: Llewellyn Publications, 1999

Morgan, Keith. *Magick for Lovers*. London: Pentacle Enterprises, 1993

Morrison, Dorothy. *Everyday Magic: Spells and Rituals for Modern Living*. St. Paul, MN: Llewellyn Publications, 1998

Morrison, Sarah Lyddon. *The Modern Witch's Spellbook*. Secaucus, NJ: Citadel Press, a Division of Lyle Stuart, Inc., 1971

Owusu, Heike. *Voodoo Rituals*. New York: Sterling Publishing Company, Inc., 2000

Pelton, Robert. *Voodoo Charms & Talismans*. Plainview, NY: Original Publications, 1997

Riva, Anna. *The Modern Herbal Spellbook: The Magical Uses of Herbs*. Toluca Lake, CA: International Imports, 1974

Riva, Anna. *Voodoo Handbook of Cult Secrets*. Toluca Lake, CA: International Imports, 1991

Slater, Herman. *The Magickal Formulary*. New York: Magickal Childe, Inc., 1981

Starhawk. *The Spiral Dance: A Rebirth of the Ancient Religion of the Great Goddess*. New York: Harper & Row, 1979

Teish, Luisah. *Jambalaya*. New York: HarperSanFrancisco, a division of HarperCollins Publishers, 1985

Turlington, Shannon R. *The Complete Idiot's Guide to Voodoo*. Indianapolis: Alpha Books, 2002

Waring, Philippa. *A Dictionary of Omens and Superstitions*. London: Souvenir Press, 1978

Index

Black peppercorns, 207
Blue balls, 141, 142
Blue Uncrossing Bath, 142–143
Body cavities, 61–63
  chest cavity, 63
  head cavity, 62–63
  stomach cavity, 63
Bourbon, 11, 191, 202
Bread braid, 89
Business dealings gone bad,
  162–164
  Mary Caliendo's Runic
    Business Hex, 162–164
Buttocks, inserting pins in, 201

C

Cain and Abel, 24
Candles
  in accessorizing poppet, 54
  anointing, 107, 112
  in Black Candle Banishing, 208
  in Blue Uncrossing Bath, 142
  in creating poppet's assistant,
    67–69
  in Crossroads Curse, 221–222
  in Curse Unraveling Ritual, 149
  in Empty Wallet Hex, 185
  in Get Out of My Life Hex,
    182, 184
  in Gimme Gumption Spell,
    11–13
  in Hex of the Nine-Patch,
    196–198
  in IRS Audit Hex, 199–200
  in Kiss Ass Curse, 230–231
  in Living Hell Hex, 225
  in Mary Caliendo's Vermin
    Hexing Spell, 226–228
  to obtain the love of a specific
    person, 190–191

  in Opposing Attorney Hex,
    173–174
  in Poppet Activation Ritual,
    69–70
  in Red Brick Victory Spell,
    171–172
  to relieve your enemy of
    personal power, 203
  in reversing the curse, 127,
    133–136, 138, 142, 149
  in safe-guarding from future
    curses, 138
  in Serial Rapist Go to Hell
    Spell, 177
  size of, 133
  in spell to stop sexual
    harassment, 213, 215
  in Swifting Ritual, 134–136
  in Witch's Bottle Hex, 224–225
Castor bean, 120
Cauldron, 21, 72, 102, 149–150,
  162, 163, 164, 186, 198, 210,
  225
Cayenne pepper, 89, 114
Celtic curse, 22–23
Cemetery Entrance Incantation, 29
Cemetery visits
  Cemetery Entrance Incantation,
    29
  digging up dirt, 30–36
  *Midnight in the Garden of
    Good and Evil*, 25
  Queen of the Dead (Oya), 27–29
  respect for the dead, 26–27
  spirits in, dealing with, 36–37
Chain stitch, 83
Chango Oil, 111, 116
Chaos, mayhem, and confusion,
  165–170
  Crow Feather Discord Hex, 170

About the Author

Dubbed by *Publishers Weekly* as "a witch to watch," Dorothy Morrison is the award-winning author of numerous books on the Ancient Arts and their application to modern life. She's won several awards for her writing and has become a favorite of readers and critics from all walks of life. Some say it's because of the easily appreciated conversational tone she applies to her work. Others say it's her down-to-earth and humorous approach to the subject matter. But regardless of the debate, all agree on one thing: whether in her writing or her interaction with the public, it's Morrison's personal style that makes her memorable. And it's that same sort of charm and grace that has some folks calling her "The Julia Sugarbaker of Paganism."

A practicing Witch since the early seventies, Morrison is an elder of the Georgian Tradition of Wicca and an initiate of the RavenMyst Circle Tradition. Formal training and group memberships aside, though, her true focus has always been on the use of magic and its practical application to everyday living; so much so, in fact, that she created the effective but easy-to-use *Wicked Witch Mojo* and *Hexology* occult product lines.

Morrison currently lives a magical life near New Orleans with her husband, Mark, and their black Lab, Dixie. She is the proprietress and sole operator of *Wicked Witch Studios (www.wickedwitchstudios.com)*, an online store specializing in handcrafted items designed for Witches of discriminating taste, which not only serve several thousand individual customers on a regular basis, but also approximately fifty retail stores nationwide.

To Our Readers

Weiser Books, an imprint of Red Wheel/Weiser, publishes books across the entire spectrum of occult, esoteric, speculative, and New Age subjects. Our mission is to publish quality books that will make a difference in people's lives without advocating any one particular path or field of study. We value the integrity, originality, and depth of knowledge of our authors.

Our readers are our most important resource, and we appreciate your input, suggestions, and ideas about what you would like to see published.

Visit our website at *www.redwheelweiser.com* to learn about our upcoming books and free downloads, and be sure to go to *www.redwheelweiser.com/newsletter* to sign up for newsletters and exclusive offers.

You can also contact us at *info@rwwbooks.com* or at

Red Wheel/Weiser, LLC
65 Parker Street, Suite 7
Newburyport, MA 01950